The Secrets of Advertising to Gen Y Consumers

The Secrets of Advertising to Gen Y Consumers

Aiden Livingston

Self-Counsel Press
(a division of)
International Self-Counsel Press Ltd.
USA   Canada

Self-Counsel Press acknowledges the financial support of the Government of Canada through the Canada Book Fund (CBF) for our publishing activities.

Printed in Canada.

First edition: 2010

Library and Archives Canada Cataloguing in Publication

Livingston, Aiden

    Secrets of advertising to Gen Y consumers / Aiden Livingston.

ISBN 978-1-77040-034-4

    1. Young adult consumers. 2. Marketing. 3. Generation Y--Attitudes. I. Title.

HF5415.32.L59 2010   658.8'340842   C2009-905732-8

Cover and Inside Image
Copyright©iStockphoto/Happy young men and women standing together/Yuri_Arcurs

Mixed Sources
Product group from well-managed forests, and other controlled sources
www.fsc.org Cert no. SW-COC-002358
© 1996 Forest Stewardship Council
FSC

Self-Counsel Press
(a division of)
International Self-Counsel Press Ltd.

1704 North State Street
Bellingham, WA 98225
USA

1481 Charlotte Road
North Vancouver, BC V7J 1H1
Canada

CONTENTS

three

KNOW THY ENEMY: INFILTRATING THE THOUGHTS OF GEN Y

four

SELLING THE STEAK NOT THE SIZZLE: WHY SENSATIONALIZED MARKETING DOESN'T WORK WITH GEN Y

five

SMALL IS THE NEW BIG: GEN Y'S ROLE IN THE RISE OF NICHE MARKETS

This book is dedicated to —

My Mom, Darlene Livingston, who always believed in me, no matter how crazy my ideas were. Her constant support has made everything possible; she is an inspiration who I am proud to call my friend, and blessed to call my mother.

My sister, Vanessa Livingston, whose caring and compassionate nature makes her a person I admire and I feel fortunate knowing that no matter what she will always have my back.

NOTICE TO READERS

Laws are constantly changing. Every effort is made to keep this publication as current as possible. However, the author, the publisher, and the vendor of this book make no representations or warranties regarding the outcome or the use to which the information in this book is put and are not assuming any liability for any claims, losses, or damages arising out of the use of this book. The reader should not rely on the author or the publisher of this book for any professional advice. Please be sure that you have the most recent edition.

ACKNOWLEDGMENTS

Sir Isaac Newton once stated, "If I have seen further it is only by standing on the shoulders of giants." I can say with confidence that I have been fortunate to stand on the shoulders of many giants.

I have had many individuals in my life whom advanced my understanding and helped me progress far beyond what I may have been able to without them. For the sake of brevity I can't begin to name them all, but I am confident they know who they are. However, all the education and information in the world could potentially sit dormant in my cerebral cortex if not for the constant support and encouragement of my close friends and family, especially the constant support I receive from my mother, Darlene Livingston. I am fairly sure I have taken many years off her life as she worries more about me more than I do.

I would be remiss if I didn't pay homage to the individuals who literally made this book a reality. I am eternally grateful to Eileen Velthuis and everyone else at Self-Counsel Press, who have always been so prompt as well as professional and had enough faith in me to publish this book. I would like to thank my delightful editor, Tanya Howe, for making me sound smarter than I really am, and for keeping my jokes tasteful.

I also would like to thank the many wonderful editors from around the world for whom I have had the pleasure to write. Lorri Freifeld from *Training/Sales and Marketing Management Magazine* and her wiener dog,

Noel, whom I feel as if I have already met; Julie Lynn of *Visibility Magazine* who has always been so thoughtful and remembered to send me a copy of any magazine in which my stories appeared; Kylie Flavell from *Marketing* magazine who was so pleasant and came up with a great article idea.

My name may be the only one on the cover, but ultimately this book was only possible because of all the aforementioned individuals, and I am forever appreciative to every last one of them.

INTRODUCTION

The problem with trying to communicate with an individual from another generation is it is a lot like trying to talk with someone from a foreign country, except the variations are less obvious. Most people instinctively realize the difficulty in trying to portray ideas to an individual from, say, Thailand. First, people see the language barrier; the Thais may not understand what you are trying to express if they don't speak English. Second, most can appreciate a cultural divergence. If a person grew up in Thailand, it is very likely he or she has different priorities and views than someone from Florida. There is literally a plethora of minor nuisances that can further impede communication between individuals from different countries. Most people are aware of these differences when dealing with people from overseas.

By contrast, most people fail to realize that the same obstacles exist when trying to reach an individual from another generation. People confuse proximity for familiarity. "Surely, a person that lives on the same street as me should be the same as me," one may justify. However, cultural deviations can be formed by temporal separations as easily as they can be from geographical separations.

Many of the obstacles we might expect in dealing with an individual from Thailand can be extrapolated to a generational frame of reference. For example, even though two generations speak English, most can appreciate that they don't necessarily speak it in the exact same way. The cliché of a parent trying in vain to incorporate his or her children's slang is ubiquitous within sitcoms and Hollywood movies for its comedic value. That is, of course, without even beginning to discuss the enigmatic code that was born from texting or SMS messaging.

Furthermore, anyone with children can appreciate that priorities and views can be very different despite living in close proximity. Differing opinions on perceived priorities is yet another example of a cultural cliché. Ironically, we all seem aware of the cultural differences inherent to different generations and yet many businesses fail to acknowledge the importance of these dissimilarities in formulating their marketing plans.

This book is a means to bridging the gap between generations. I explain the different values and perceptions so that people can more accurately construct advertising campaigns that reach Gen Y consumers in the most effective and efficient way possible. Many other authors have delved headfirst into this topic, and many are brilliant writers who make cunning observations. However, at the end of the day the Achilles' heel of these books is that they are based on observations. When the problem is a cultural deviation, it is only prudent to have a member of the studied culture provide insight into the issue. To do otherwise is to fail to address the root of the problem.

I make my deductions based on my life and my experiences, not from what I have observed in an individual from a foreign culture. This is ultimately the greatest advantage to this book for the reader. My conclusions are not subject to error in interpretation because the culture I explain is my own; I live it every day. My every interaction in the day recapitulates the principles I discuss, whether it is a conversation with a friend about what movie to see tonight, or my internal dialogue when I go to make a purchase. It is in exploring my own actions and those of my peers that I am able to produce an invaluable resource for anyone who seeks to truly understand how to best reach Gen Y consumers.

one
WHY CARE ABOUT GENERATION Y?

Why should businesses care about one single generation? Why should they restructure their entire marketing model to cater to one group? The reason is because the methods and tactics that can be utilized to reach Gen Y represent the future of marketing. New technologies and an ever-changing world have assured that we can never go back to how things used to be. The paradigm has shifted and the difficulties most advertisers are facing in trying to reach customers stand only to get worse with each following generation.

Gen Y just so happens to be the generation who was born and raised during this major technological revolution. In a way, studying how to reach and market to Gen Y is in fact a lesson on how advertising will look in the future. The techniques discussed in this book will eventually be explored and refined so thoroughly that they will represent the new standard in marketing. It is beneficial to learn the lessons Gen Y has to teach now, or risk falling behind in a highly competitive, globalized world.

1. Who Is Gen Y?

As a member of Gen Y myself, allow me a few moments to make our collective introduction. Members of Gen Y were born between 1982 and 2002 (exact years vary depending on who you ask), which explains their other nickname, the Millennials. Another nickname is the Echo Boomers, which is in relation to the fact that they are usually the children of the Baby Boomer generation. They have also been referred to as Net Generation, Dot-Com Generation, and Trophy Generation; however, in my opinion most of these names are pretty lame and hopelessly uncreative, so I will stick with Gen Y.

In the United States alone Gen Y represents more than 80 million people, a number that is likely to grow over time with immigration. Gen Y spends more than 200 billion dollars a year in the US alone and have a major influence on their parents' spending habits, the spending behemoths called the Baby Boomers.

2. Twenty-First Century Digital Boy

Gen Y has grown up in a world bathed in technology. I often can't help but to look at the world my parents grew up in only to be filled with pity and empathy. I can recall many conversations with my mother, whose exact age will remain a mystery for the sake of my own safety, but suffice it to say she is a Baby Boomer.

"So I can understand that you didn't have cell phones, but no answering machines either? What would you do if the person you were trying to reach wasn't home?" I queried. "Just call back another time and hope you catch the person or that someone else would be home so he or she could write a note to get the person to call you back," my mother replied flippantly. How barbaric, I thought: this seemed to me as reliable a method of communication as homing pigeons.

Most of Gen Y has had cell phones as long as we can remember, or at the very least, a pager. In fact, if on the rare occasion I leave my cell phone at home by accident, I experience what I feel is the same grief and helplessness of an avid jogger who just had a cast put on!

Perhaps most unsettling is the thought of a world without the Internet. The very concept sends chills up the spines of many Gen Ys. Not being able to check on my Facebook account, or Google my every whim or question is a withdrawal-inducing scenario. Moreover, the concept of not having any Internet at all is simply befuddling to most of Gen Y. The idea of having to go to an actual library to look up something, or the tedium of trying to write a research paper at a library having to search through individual books for information that are now available in three seconds on Google is daunting.

3. The Future Will Be More of the Same

The important thing to remember is that all generations from here on out will grow up with the same technological privileges or more, and their expectations will be just as high as Gen Y's, if not higher. Our aptitude toward instant gratification, and demanding nature will only be amplified in future generations, such as Gen Z: Imagine how someone born in 2005 will view the world in 20 years. No doubt I will have to spend time explaining to them why before MP3s we had to buy CDs and store them in a giant binder that resembled the sign-in book at Ellis Island in both its size and seemingly random nature of its entries.

Appealing to Gen Y and having them embrace your product can actually hugely affect the overall market perception of your product and your brand in general.

4. The Trickle-up Effect

It is also noteworthy that although earlier generations may not expect or demand the same level of innovation from companies, they certainly appreciate the innovations. It is not a matter of choosing to market to Gen Y at the peril of losing customers and potential clients from other age ranges. In fact, quite the opposite, the innovations needed to reach and appeal to Gen Y actually charm all generations.

Just because older generations grew up in a world where lack of technology made many of the new marketing avenues impossible, doesn't mean they don't see the value in it. For instance, Apple has employed many new marketing techniques and has had great success establishing themselves in the minds of Gen Y; I can proudly say this book was written on a MacBook Air. However, the advertisements Apple uses to appeal to younger consumers also has a poignant effect on older generations. Many of my Gen Y friends' parents own MacBooks and love them. Not only because MacBooks work well, but also because of what owning a Mac says about you to other people. It screams young and hip, and let's face it, the young and the hip aren't the only ones trying to project that image. In reality, Baby Boomers seem more susceptible to the need to appear young and hip than their kids do.

Appealing to Gen Y and having them embrace your product can actually hugely affect the overall market perception of your product and your brand in general. This in turn gives you a huge advantage in not just reaching Baby Boomers, but having a heavy influence on whether or not they actually purchase your product.

Furthermore, one thing most people fail to consider is how large of an impact Gen Y has over their parents' purchases. Gen Y prides itself on being able to "research" and deduce what is the best purchase to be made. We go to online forums, read reviews, ask our friends, and look over numerous other sources of information before finally making what we believe is the most informed decision.

Perhaps even more tenacious than our research habits is our propensity for bragging about what smart consumers we are. We don't do all that work for nothing; if nobody knows how brilliant we are, what is the point of being brilliant at all? Unlike a tree falling in the woods, we insist on being heard.

As a result most Baby Boomer parents pained with the decision of a new purchase typically consult their Gen Y kids. It is a beautifully symbiotic relationship; we get to flex our cognitive muscles and our parents get to shrug the responsibility of having to make a difficult decision in a marketplace that is flooded with confusing choices.

5. The Ones Pulling All the Strings

Most people tend to underestimate the influence Gen Y has over their parents. However, they forget the different dynamic that exists between Baby Boomer parents and their Gen Y kids. It is much different than the relationship the Baby Boomers had with their parents. Most of Gen Y talks to their parents regularly; I talk to my mom almost daily.

Moreover, much of Gen Y still lives with their parents: A practice I don't particularly condone, but nonetheless it has become more common than not. It is not uncommon for even the oldest of Gen Y, now 27, to still be milking the parental cash cow. Many get their names on advanced college degrees before getting their name on an apartment lease.

However, even the members of Gen Y who do manage to move out remain very close to their parents, they talk frequently, and still spend a lot of time together. Most even still vacation with their parents and not just out of obligation. The reason is more so than any generation before it: Gen Y and their parents are often good friends. It is because of this closeness that Gen Y has a huge impact over their parents' purchasing decisions. So by marketing to and attracting Gen Y customers you will actually be having a huge impact on Baby Boomers' purchasing power as well. Those two groups combined constitute a majority of all the purchasing power in North America.

Ultimately the main reason to learn to market to Gen Y is because they are the future. Like it or not, a threshold has been crossed and there is no going back. Companies have the choice to learn and restructure accordingly now, while Gen Y is still relatively young and still hasn't grown into its full potential, or choose to wait. The problem is that, as with learning anything new, it takes time, so you can take steps now to learn and adapt, or linger until the future makes your old model totally invalid and then struggle to try to catch up to the competition, which most likely won't be possible.

Gen Y's ideas don't simply represent a new method in doing business with them, as much as how business will be done in the future. After all, the old techniques for marketing were fine in the early part of the twentieth century, since the reach to the market and methods were limited by technology. However, these days methods are limited only by the limits of the companies own imaginations and their sense of innovation in exploring this exciting new frontier.

At the end of the day, using outdated methods when newer methods are available at a lower cost and greater efficiency, is not only foolish it is dangerous; like storing meat on the windowsill when you have a perfectly good refrigerator. You might be able to get away with it for a little bit, but eventually it will catch up with you.

two
THE RISE AND FALL OF TRADITIONAL MARKETING

Most regard traditional marketing with the reverence you would grant a religion, as though it has been around forever and will continue on unchanged well into the future. The truth is traditional marketing techniques most advertisers rely on have only really been in practice for less then 100 years, with a majority of the practice having only been standardized and perfected within the last 50 years. Perhaps since people tend to mistakenly believe that traditional advertising has existed for so long, they are likely to cling to the principles of traditional advertising when crafting their marketing campaigns and budgets.

However, Gen Y is all but immune to many of these traditional techniques. To actually reach Gen Y, companies must use new and innovative techniques. In many ways the rise of these traditional marketing methods from obscurity to the golden standards is being mirrored by the rise of modern advertising techniques. So it is important to learn the history of traditional marketing, if you are to understand why and how advertising will change in the future.

What is traditional marketing? Essentially, traditional marketing is paid ads being shown on billboards, in newspapers, in magazines, or in catalogs. Paid ads can also be aired between programs on television and on the radio. When you hear it put in plain English, it is almost remarkable how uncreative and unexciting the traditional advertising model sounds. Especially since most people in the advertising industry pride themselves on being creative people, but let's face it: Following this format is about as creative as throwing a sheet over yourself on Hallowe'en and going as a ghost.

It is also important to note with all the formats listed in this chapter as traditional marketing, virtually none of them have any chance at reaching a member of Gen Y.

1. Billboards

The oldest of the advertising techniques is billboard advertising. In fact, as early as in Egyptian times merchants used signs to try and draw more customers to their business; though the current form of billboard advertising we all think of when we consider the concept of outdoor advertising is pretty far removed from hanging a sheet of papyrus paper on a wall announcing mummification services. Therefore, it is safe to say the actual practice of billboard advertising used today was developed much later.

In the early part of the twentieth century, the first freeway billboard ads began to appear. Billboard ads were quite popular at the time because most products were advertised and sold on a local level. It made sense to put a giant billboard alongside the main freeway most of your local consumers used to get home. The practice worked so well the Feds had to step in and regulate it.

I, for one, would be excited to use the mile-long billboards referenced in Ray Bradbury's futuristic tale *Fahrenheit 451*. But of course "The Man" had to step in and ruin our good time by passing the 1965 Highway Beautification Act, which strictly regulated the size and number of billboards that could be used. This was great news for those who owned billboards because rates went through the roof, and even today billboards are still predominantly only used by huge conglomerates. Therefore, billboards are well out of the budget of most small- and mid-sized companies.

2. Catalogs

The next traditional marketing method to develop was catalog marketing. In the early part of the twentieth century many purchases were made using catalogs, which helped to establish many of the retail giants. Even today IKEA uses catalogs as a staple in its advertising presence. Catalogs still manage to be useful in killing time when you are waiting for a doctor, or for covering ugly rings left on your coffee table from coasterless cups.

However, in modern times of online catalogs with quick search options, their paper counterparts are becoming a little outdated. Much like using a phone book to look up a number, sure, it is still possible but with Google a few clicks away, why bother searching through a huge confusing book? As this trend continues catalogs will eventually be literally worth less than the paper they are printed on.

3. Newspapers

Another printed marketing form that is steadily losing steam in the face of more efficient digital competition is the newspaper. The first paid ad to appear in a newspaper was in the French paper *La Presse* in 1836. The ads were used to offset the price of printing the newspapers and allowed the publishers to lower their price. The model was quickly adapted by other papers around the world, and it is still the business model used by most newspapers today.

The original ads were very basic and straightforward, stating the facts. They did not include any fancy typeset or illustrations, so the system of newspaper advertising used today was actually developed during the early part of the twentieth century. However, the current low readership means most newspapers around the world are struggling to stay in the black. If they are having trouble keeping the doors open, they are probably losing prominence as an advertising form.

Gen Y seems poised to put the final nail in the printed newspaper's coffin. The majority of Gen Ys get their news from online sources such as bloggers. Many speculate that printed newspapers may come to an end within the next ten years; a fact which depresses me, because how else am I supposed to look intelligent when in public? Moreover, what will I wrap breakables in when packing?

4. Magazines

Closely akin to the dilemma facing most newspapers, most magazines are slowly losing readership and are having trouble staying profitable against online sources that spend nothing on printing and distribution. Printing is especially problematic for most magazines because of the extra cost of the colorful, glossy pages as opposed to inexpensive newspaper print. Magazines have been slowly seeking to niche themselves, in order to maintain readership, and to make them more targeted for marketers trying to reach a specific audience.

Yet once again in the face of online competition that has no printing expenses, and can distribute specialized content to readers worldwide at no added distribution cost, magazines will continue to struggle into the future. They will especially struggle amongst the Gen Y community, because when it comes to paying $8 for a magazine, I find myself thinking, no way because I can get it for free online. It is this mind-set that will be

The majority of Gen Ys get their news from online sources such as bloggers.

the undoing of much of the printed world. It will be just too hard to compete with digital counterparts that have fewer expenses and can still make money from selling ad space. The more efficient model has and always will dominate, given a long enough timeframe.

5. Dethroning Media Royalty

The traditional marketing formats that have dominated the marketplace for the last 50 years would undoubtedly be radio and television advertising. A vast majority of many advertising budgets are dwindled on these two resources. Yet much like their printed counterparts, these two formats are in serious jeopardy, specifically as a result of the changing habits of Gen Y. Ultimately these advertising mediums were the cutting edge technologies of their day, but now newer and better technologies are set to knock them from their pedestals.

5.1 Radio

Broadcast radio was first started and used by radio manufacturers as a way of selling more radios. They figured broadcasting free radio shows was a good way to convince consumers to make the pretty substantial investment to buy a radio. Keep in mind this was when radios were still the size of kitchen hutches and lurked forebodingly in the corner of people's living rooms. It wasn't until marketers started to see just how much time the average family spent listening to their radios that they finally realized the potential for using this new technology as a way to have their message reach the masses. The effect was immediate and substantial, and soon after most major advertisers saw the advantage in sponsoring short radio shows to receive mention of their product. In fact, this is actually where the term soap opera came from: It's the result of soap manufacturers sponsoring short daytime radio dramas. The shows were recurring and would draw listeners in on a daily basis to hear the next dramatic turn of events.

The format worked quite well to establish products in the minds of customers, and very much influenced purchasing. Keep in mind this was a time when most people tended to grant more credence to what they heard on the radio. After all, it was during this time that Orson Welles did a short radio show in which he read HG Wells' *The War of the Worlds*, and caused mass hysteria. When Steven Spielberg retold the same tale with millions of dollars in special effects and big name actors, he could hardly even motivate Gen Y to go to an afternoon matinee, much less form a riotous mob. So the sensitivity of the listening public to lend credibility to anything they hear on the radio has dwindled, to say the least. That is if they are even listening to the radio at all.

Personally I never listen to the radio. For all the years Gen Y has been able to drive, we have had CD players in our cars, which enabled us to listen to our music collection on the go. Albeit, the effectiveness of the CDs begins to wane as they get scratched up. More recently, people have been able to listen to their iPods when they drive anywhere. People can either use a small device that transmits a radio frequency from their iPod to the car stereo system, or, many new vehicles have jacks that can directly plug in the iPod, especially any of the vehicles that are being deliberately marketed to Gen Y. Vehicle manufacturers were able to see the trend that the vast majority would rather listen to their own iPod collection than some radio show, packed with dumb commercials and mindless chitchat. Once again going into the future, the old technology (of radio) will be continually superseded by the more efficient technology (of iPods). Many people, if given the choice, like the option of listening to thousands of songs they picked as their favorites, rather than listening to a radio program that only plays some songs they like, with a lot of commercials between those songs, and having to endure some deejay ramble on about his date over the weekend. The decision seems pretty obvious.

5.2 Television

Having saved the best for last, let me introduce the most prominent form of traditional marketing: television advertising. TV ads still cost the most money and this is where most advertisers spend the majority of their budgets. For example, for a 30-second commercial during the Super Bowl a company will spend around 2.7 million dollars. Which I will admit of all the occasions, people specifically watch the Super Bowl for the game and the funny commercials. But at the end of the day, how effective are the ads? I mean, who is watching the Super Bowl and sees a Budweiser commercial, and immediately jumps up to go buy some Bud Light? These spectators are not in purchasing mode, they are in sports-watching mode.

The start of TV advertising is much different than the model we tend to think of today. In fact, it used to be that only one company would sponsor an entire show, and the show would be named accordingly. Who can forget such favorites as the Kraft Television Theatre or the Texaco Star Theater? This was the standard TV advertising way until the 1950s when an NBC executive named Sylvester "Pat" Weaver introduced the "magazine format." The idea was to divide the cost of sponsoring a show to lower costs on advertisers, and enable networks to make higher advertising revenue. The concept resulted in the commercial breaks with which we are all too painfully familiar these days.

However, much like radio, this format is threatened by many emerging technologies, one of which is undoubtedly TiVo and other Digital

Just like the innovators of the twentieth century did, it is still important to embrace new technology and incorporate it quickly.

Video Recorders (DVRs). I personally love my TiVo, but it is a nightmare for those who wish to advertise on TV. Now people can watch their favorite TV show and fast-forward through the ads. This is the equivalent of when a mouse figures out how to get the cheese without setting off the trap. Yet once again in the mind of most Gen Ys who grew up in an "instant" world, it seems absurd to have to wait around all night for your favorite show to come on, and then to have to be subjected to relentless amounts of boring commercials. Why bother when we can just digitally record it, watch it when we are ready, and fast-forward through the commercials? Like all other examples, the most efficient technology will always prevail with Gen Y.

Moreover, even if one doesn't own a DVR, virtually all TV shows are available online and can be watched with either no commercials whatsoever, or simply a banner ad displayed in the background. In comparison to waiting for your show to start and having to sit through ads, this is a much more palatable system and most networks are even beginning to kowtow to the emerging importance of the Internet, and making their programs available through their websites for online viewing. In a way they are participating in their own demise. It was summed up best by cartoon character Homer Simpson when he bought his first TiVo. He was fast-forwarding through the commercials and he said something like, "I spit on your grave, commercial-sponsored television!"

Ultimately, the traditional marketing techniques most advertisers still cling to became popular because they were the technological innovations of their day. They were the cutting edge strategies for reaching customers in the most efficient and tactical way. However, let's face it, TV and radio haven't been cutting edge technology since James Dean was around, and nobody has been impressed by the idea of the newspaper since people were using candles to light the way to their outhouses. Just like the innovators of the twentieth century did, it is still important to embrace new technology and incorporate it quickly.

I am sure there were companies in the 1950s that said, "Aw, this TV advertising is just a Baby Boomer fad, let's just stick to what we are doing now." I would name companies but let's face it, any company that didn't adjust to the emerging technologies of the 1950s has probably gone out of business by now.

We now find ourselves on the brink of many new technologies that stand poised to change the world of marketing all over again. You can either adjust and learn to market to this newest generation using the technologies they actually use, or continue to spend money to place ads where they will never be seen.

three
KNOW THY ENEMY: INFILTRATING THE THOUGHTS OF GEN Y

The collective experience of any generation forms their shared values and perceptions. Every dramatic event molds mentalities, and advancement of technology sets the standards of expectations.

The assignation of such prolific civil right leaders as John F. Kennedy (JFK) and Dr. Martin Luther King Jr. helped to form a generation of progressive-thinking hippies. Not content with their parents' status quo they sought, and often succeeded, to enact social change, through mass protest. The events they witnessed growing up established a rebellious mind-set in the Baby Boomer generation. Had they grown up in a less turbulent time, they may not have been so apt to open and constant rebellion.

When most Baby Boomers were entering their impressionable teenage years it was the 1960s, which was a time of great and swift social windfall. Perceptions on equality and human rights that had been virtually untouched for generations came crashing down in the span of one decade. Women were finally seen as equals, and not as stereotyped into gender roles. African Americans were finally able to realize many of the rights that had been denied to them for so long. In fact, the first African American president, Barack Obama, is a Baby Boomer.

During Gen Y's more formative years much of the dust had settled on social change. The new revolution was a technological revolution. It admittedly was not as cool as the revolution in the '60s; instead of bra

This push toward interconnectivity on a global scale can be exploited for the purposes of marketing and can build brand awareness faster and more efficiently than could be done any other time in history.

burnings, we had adolescent boys who spent so much time sedentary and eating junk food in front of computer screens that they ended up needing bras! The hippies sought to change the world and we sought to change the *World of Warcraft*. Even though our revolution may not have left us with anything as cool as CCR or John Fogerty songs playing over clips of Vietnam, it was ultimately much more dramatic and world changing far beyond what anyone could have ever imagined!

1. A Truly Interconnected World

In keeping with our parents' hippie mind-sets, the world of Gen Y has become surprisingly unified. I have spent years traveling around the world. I have been on all the continents, and the thing I have found most amazing is how unified Gen Y's world truly is.

As of the writing this book I have been in 30 different countries. Now I do try to learn a little of the local tongue, nothing mindblowing, usually just niceties such as, "How are you?" and "Cheers" and "Thank you." I learned enough that when I meet someone from that country again I can impress him or her. You may have noticed though that none of the phrases I learned have any chance of getting me the basic necessities I need to stay alive. You can say "Salud" till you are blue in the face in Argentina, but nobody will bring you a steak. How did I manage not to starve to death in a Moroccan gutter during my years overseas? The reason is if you meet anyone who is a Gen Y member anywhere in the world, odds are they can speak English. Think for a second how profound that is. The result is many Gen Ys can communicate with each other. I have had many dinners where more than ten different countries from three continents are represented at the table. My mini-UN dinner parties aside, this serves as an exemplification of the globalized world that was ushered in during Gen Y's formative years. Now add to the equation the inclination, or rather addiction to social networking, and you can see what an amazingly intertwined global community Gen Y is. This is a very important fact to remember because this push toward interconnectivity on a global scale can be exploited for the purposes of marketing and can build brand awareness faster and more efficiently than could be done any other time in history.

2. Immune to Traditional Marketing

In a way it is almost impossible to reach Gen Y not using new methods. It is because Gen Y grew up in a world where target marketing was the norm, and as a result they have become very desensitized to traditional marketing techniques. Since the 1980s, when Gen Y was born, an individual going about his or her routine is subjected to more than 3,500 advertisements daily. Considering Gen Y has literally been inundated with these marketing techniques since they were toddlers, how many of the ads do you think actually get through to them? They became immune out of necessity.

The way most advertisers approached this problem was to inundate them with even more traditional marketing campaigns. The rationale behind this is rather dizzying, the equivalent of trying to binge eat until you are skinny. Out of desperation most advertisers became even more invasive, like obsessive stalkers, doing whatever it took to garnish even a moment's worth of attention. We responded by filing a restraining order stating that the stalk-you-tisers had to stay 50 yards away at all times and could only show their ads on TV that we TiVo and then fast-forward through, and radio stations we never listen to. The fundamental flaw for the advertisers is the same mistake most stalkers make, a failure to communicate and actually understand the desires of the one you are pursuing. Metaphorically speaking, we only wanted to talk and get to know Brand X better, but then Brand X started calling 50 times a day to tell us how much it needs us, and freaked us out.

The point is, you must work on being the kind of company Gen Y can love if you really want to reach them. You need to establish what is important to them, and reach them in a way that is appropriate and noninvasive.

3. Doing a Common Thing Uncommonly Well

An example of a company that Gen Y loves is Threadless.com. I recommend checking out the site if you are not already familiar with it. Threadless.com sells t-shirts; not exactly a groundbreaking product, but like Henry John Heinz, the founder of the famous Heinz Ketchup, so eloquently stated, "to do a common thing uncommonly well brings success."

How does Threadless.com peddle garments to make them so appealing to Gen Y? Well, the primary difference between Threadless.com and other traditional apparel companies is Threadless.com's customers are also their designers and marketers. Essentially, how it works is graphic designers from all around the world submit their best designs to the site for other users to vote on. The shirts that receive the highest rating get a cash reward and the designs become available for purchase through the website. The designers create the very best designs they can so they can proudly display their work to the Threadless.com community. The shirts are even linked to the designers' profiles giving added incentive to become one of the top designers.

User-generated content sites have enjoyed so much success among the Gen Y demographic; it plays on a fundamental principle that both motivates and infatuates most members of Gen Y.

To get a higher vote count what would you imagine is the first thing any designer might do after submitting a design? They go on to every social networking site they can and try to direct as many people as they possibly can to Threadless.com to vote for their shirt, so they can get a higher rating and possibly win the cash reward. Does Gen Y mind taking up the majority of the duties of designing a new product and then promoting the product for free on Threadless.com? Quite the opposite; they love doing so. They feel they are actually part of the site, and they see themselves as members of an online community; not as its exploited free workers.

3.1 Gen Y loves to show off talent

Threadless.com illustrates quite well several important points to remember in trying to market to Gen Y. First, Gen Y prides themselves on their creativity, often in the face of having no discernible talent. Seemingly, any members of Gen Y with sufficient upper-body strength to lift a single-lens reflex (SLR) camera fancy themselves as professional photographers.

The statistic increases exponentially if they are overseas at the time. I find myself constantly dodging tourists who feel quite content holding up crowded sidewalks to painstakingly get their "perfect shot." Then they proudly post massive collections of these uninspired pictures on their Facebook or Flixster profiles. Friends then leave comments, and the whole vicious cycle continues.

The actual merit of some of these creations notwithstanding, it is important to note that Gen Y loves expressing itself, and reviewing and commenting on other people's creations. This is why user-generated content sites have enjoyed so much success among the Gen Y demographic; it plays on a fundamental principle that both motivates and infatuates most members of Gen Y.

3.2 Gen Y loves a sense of community

Furthermore, Threadless.com gives Gen Y something else they constantly crave: a sense of community. The need to belong to something bigger than themselves is probably a by-product of an overall sense of interconnectivity. Gen Y loves to build themselves up within a community, and have a strong desire to belong. They enjoy seeing comments, often from complete strangers. They proudly display a Facebook page that has well over 1,000 friends and yet they might not be able to get four people to come over to their house for a game of Monopoly.

In this way, it is a real quantity over quality complex. Gen Y would rather have their profile seen by ten virtual strangers than two people they have been friends with since grade school. So any site like Threadless.com that gives them the chance to reach out and connect with more and more people, especially people with similar interests, is quickly embraced by Gen Y.

It is important to note that there must be a degree of similar interest. Online communities don't generally congregate for the sake of congregating; they congregate because they are all members of the North America Congregators' Advocates Association. If you are unfamiliar with all the great things this very fictitious organization is doing I recommend subscribing to their online newsletter. The point being, a common goal or interest is essential to achieving an online community that Gen Y will both embrace and market for you.

At the end of the day, if you want to achieve the kind of unprecedented success Threadless.com was able to and become an overnight sensation, it is important to remember that modern marketing has to be more of a dialogue then a monologue. It is not enough to simply talk at your customers these days, they expect more, especially Gen Y. Because of modern technology this conversation has become relatively straightforward. Companies have the chance to give their customers a voice and to induce communities based around their products or services learn what their customers actually want. However, much like a staunch paroled stalker, they have just been paroled, and are back to thinking of over-the-top gestures they can do to just make Gen Y love them. Showing up at all hours of the night with gifts that Gen Y neither wants nor will accept. It is important to break the cycle and learn to communicate with Gen Y, and discover how to reach them in a way that they will appreciate.

You must learn to fill Gen Y's needs and discover what they want. Much like the actual dating world, this can be a tedious process, but it is a necessary process if you want your company to actually be in a solid relationship with Gen Y and not be the creepy stalker calling them over and over again as they're out dating other companies and ignoring your calls. Albert Einstein said it best when he said insanity is the act of "doing the same thing over and over again and expecting different results."

four
SELLING THE STEAK NOT THE SIZZLE: WHY SENSATIONALIZED MARKETING DOESN'T WORK WITH GEN Y

An old marketing adage once said, "Sell the sizzle, not the steak." Which is to say, focus on the intangibles of a product over the product itself. A good example would be car commercials that sell the lifestyle and image of a car instead of focusing on the actual car. A car company will show a vehicle full of supermodels, which is to imply that if you buy this over-priced gas guzzler, supermodels will want to ride with you. I am not sure if this tactic ever really worked on anyone; part of me hopes no one could be that naive and gullible.

To Gen Y these commercials have the opposite effect. Instead of per-suading them to buy, the ads feel patronizing and silly especially when the product the car companies are pitching quite obviously does not render the lifestyle they suggest. If the ad showed a guy buying a Ferrari and gal-livanting about town with young, attractive golddiggers, I would admit the commercial could have a point. However, when they show a guy buying a Hyundai Accent and now all the hot girls want him, it leaves me think-ing, "What kind of idiot does the advertiser take me for?" A new $5,000 car might garnish a few looks from attractive girls in a poorer country where the prospect of a guy owning any car is impressive. However, in North America, having an inexpensive entry-level car is only slightly more impressive then having an unlimited-use bus pass!

When it comes to trying to reach Gen Y, over-the-top marketing claims will have the opposite of the desired effect.

1. Sensational or Sensationalized

The practice of trying to sell the glamorized image of a product is called sensationalized marketing. This has been the standard way advertisers have tried to communicate their products to consumers throughout Gen Y's life. The advertisers try to sell the sexiness of a product, or how much better your life will be with the product.

I always have to laugh when I see commercials for Valtrex, which is a prescription medication for genital herpes. The TV commercials show people kayaking, going for hikes in scenic wilderness surroundings, or riding a double-seated bicycle down a beach boardwalk. I would joke with my friends and say, "If only we could all be so lucky as to be living with genital herpes; I mean when was the last time we took a double-seated bike out for a spin down the boardwalk?"

Another classic offender is late night infomercials. The infomercials often take the most mundane of items and then proceed to explain how this piece of kitchenware will change my life. Even before they make their outrageous claims I consider all the items I currently have in my kitchen, none of which have ever even managed to impact my life in any significant way, much less change it completely.

It is hard for me to say for sure if any of the older generations ever really appreciated these kinds of sensationalized ads that offend logic and spit in the face of common sense. I do know that when it comes to trying to reach Gen Y, over-the-top marketing claims will have the opposite of the desired effect.

2. Brainy and Boastful

The fundamental flaw in the sensationalized method of marketing is it fails to address the fact that Gen Y prides themselves on being smart and informed consumers. Any purchasing decision is preceded by enough research and analysis to make even Thomas Edison blush. We read reviews, ask questions on online forums, we consult our friends, even cross-reference prices and features on manufacturers' websites. In fact, it is interesting to see when one of my Gen Y friends, myself included, finally resolve to make a purchase. We are so inordinately proud of what a good job we did that we end up taking an undeserved sense of pride in the product.

Recently my Gen Y friend, Sara, bought a new mountain bike. Directly after ordering the bike from a local store, she came home and showed all of us online which bike she was getting. Sara then went into a rather long and boring dissertation on why this was the right bike for her needs.

"You see, the bike has extra shocks, because you know how I like to go biking in the mountains, and it has a special memory foam seat because you know how sensitive my tailbone has been since that snowboarding accident … " and so on *ad nauseam*. If you were to listen to her excessively enthusiastic diatribe, you would swear she had designed the bike herself, or at the very least was deeply involved in the manufacturing process. In reality, Sara did nothing but make the decision to buy the bike, but her enthusiasm for her purchase articulates a distinct difference in the Gen Y mind-set that most advertisers fail to address.

3. Gen Y Doesn't Mind Doing the Research

Gen Y doesn't find the process of researching products tedious or exhausting, in fact, I think we can't help but be this way. I have made snap decisions before when I was at a shop and I felt pressured to buy a product immediately by either a one-day sale, or perhaps it was the last in stock. However, the first thing I do when I get home is begin my normal research process, even after I have already made my purchase, just to make sure it was a good decision. More to the point, I want to make sure it was the "best" decision. For example, I recently bought a digital camera to replace the one that had been stolen on my travels. I had not yet done any research but I was in the mall and the siren's call of the display *Guitar Hero* video game was beckoning me in to Best Buy. After a rousing round of "Free Bird," I decided to take a gander at the cameras.

Now I had been quite happy with my previous camera and had it not been for a sticky-fingered thief, I would have been more than content to use it for another year or so. However, since I was going to have to make a new purchase, why not try to find something even better, and a super slim Casio seemed to be the perfect candidate. As luck would have it, the camera was on sale and it was the last one in the manly black finish. Were I not to buy it now I could be stuck with the red model, which bordered too closely to pink for my taste. I was stuck between a rock and a hard place. I could purchase this camera that seemingly filled all my purposes, or I could go home and research it to make sure it was the best choice and potentially go back to the store later only to be stuck with the camera color that would test the security of my masculinity. The prospect of being stuck with a fuchsia-colored camera proved too terrifying to risk, so I bought the last black one.

The first thing I did when I got home was consult the online reviews and guides. I was gutted by what I discovered. Although the camera fit all my needs, and the highly reduced price made it a compelling deal, it was not, in fact, the "best" camera I could have bought. Perhaps most insulting was that it was not quite as good as the camera it was replacing. I still

Gen Y consumers view information gathering and analyzing as an essential part of the purchasing process.

find myself looking at pictures that were taken by my old camera with a certain longing that one usually reserves for lost loves. Even though the camera adequately filled all my purposes, which are pretty minimal, I still had buyer's remorse because I could have bought an even better camera had I taken the time to research ahead of time like I normally would.

4. Information at Our Fingertips

Gen Y consumers view information gathering and analyzing as an essential part of the purchasing process. This is why sensationalized marketing techniques are so ineffective with this generation of consumers. We want to get all the available facts and decipher the information in order to make an informed decision. This is ultimately the result of growing up in an era when so much information is so readily available. We have always had the "information superhighway" at our fingertips, so this ingrained the habit, or rather craving for information in Gen Y.

By comparison, my mother hates having to do the research about a new purchase and is more than happy to shrug responsibility on to me. Many Baby Boomers would rather have the decision made for them; they find the limitless options inherent to modern day purchasing exhausting. They remember growing up in a world that wasn't so complicated, where when they needed a product they went to the local store and bought the item that most closely met their needs. Market saturation wasn't an issue in those days, and the long lists of features and personalization options were limited by manufacturers' technologies.

Even to this day you can see the difference when it comes to purchasing a laptop. I will see my friends' parents get hung up on every detail. Whether deciding what processor speed, amount of RAM, or most insignificantly the color of the laptop, Baby Boomers seem pained by having so many choices. Even the fundamental decision of Mac or PC leaves a lot of Baby Boomers scratching their heads, which to me seems ridiculous because I would go back to writing with pen and paper before I go back to a PC!

5. Growing up in a World Full of Choices

Baby Boomers like an authoritative figure helping them to make a decision. This would explain why sensationalized marketing was an effective practice for this generation. They liked having a commercial tell them definitively what was the best purchase choice for them. They didn't have to explain why this was the best choice, and the argument didn't necessarily have to make sense. Baby Boomers just liked to be reassured before making a decision, to be pointed in the right direction. It's not that Baby

Boomers are dumb or unable to research a purchase the same way Gen Y does, they simply grew up in a time when it wasn't as necessary. Their purchasing habits were formed in a different economic climate. In the 1960s and the 1970s much of the manufacturing was still done within the United States. The markets weren't flooded with hundreds of foreign manufacturers seeking to niche themselves within a marketplace.

During the 1990s to the present, markets have become constantly more and more saturated with endless variety. Increases in manufacturing technology have meant more products being developed by endless new companies from countries all over the world, which has equaled endless options and considerations for every product. The difference is Gen Y has grown up in a world of saturated markets and they are quite used to, if not expectant, of the limitless choices. We don't mind spending the extra time learning about and comparing all the features, since we have been doing this all of our lives.

I remember being only eight years old and having to weigh the pros and cons of a Super Nintendo or a Sega Genesis. I considered the graphics of the systems, plus the caliber and number of games for each system. Many of the younger video game consumers have had even tougher decisions as new systems have emerged. Now the options are the Wii, the Xbox, or the PlayStation. I pity the poor eight-year-old who is left with that decision! Deciding between only two caused me many sleepless nights and took years off my adolescent life!

6. You Must Show Gen Y You Are the Best

As opposed to our Baby Boomer parents, Gen Y doesn't want some unknown advertiser giving them a sensationalized pitch on why its product is the best fit for them without backing it up with facts. If you want Gen Y to purchase your product, you must understand how important it is for them to feel they have done their due diligence in researching the product. At the end of the day they need to know why this was the best product for them. Simply stating that it is the "best" without substantiating the claim is far more likely to irk Gen Y than to influence them.

Speaking as a person from Gen Y, we like making up our minds for ourselves. We want retailers to give the information needed to make the decision; we don't want them to make it for us. This is where the Internet can be very useful for companies. Things such as online interactive guides, forums, and user reviews allow Gen Y consumers to feel like we have made the best decision. Ultimately, we might not always make the best decision, but we just need to have consulted enough information to feel like we are making an informed decision.

If a retailer can give us the feeling that we have made the informed decision after having visited its site, read all the user-generated forums and reviews, then used an interactive guide to help us decide which features are best suited to our needs, we will undoubtedly buy the product. Why? Because we can rest easy thinking we had really looked into it and picked the "best" product.

Many companies don't like the idea of user-generated reviews on their sites because of the inevitability of negative reviews. Yet this is a mistake; in fact, the reviews humanize the opinions, and give us the feeling we have gathered all the information; good and bad. The reviews will actually positively influence Gen Y, unless the majority of the reviews are bad, at which point you should probably take a look at improving your product to better suit your customers' needs.

At the end of the day, over-the-top sensationalized marketing may have worked on previous generations who were more eager to have someone help them navigate through the limitless choices. However, Gen Y has grown up in a world where picking a toothbrush offers no less than a hundred different options, from flexible necks, gum massagers, battery power, or sonic cleaning power. I personally use anything that bears the likeness of SpongeBob, but only because I trust his integrity!

As a generation we don't view too many choices as a problem; in fact, we enjoy the opportunity to be able to take the time and pick the best product. If you are trying to reach Gen Y consumers, forget all the flair and focus on the facts.

five

SMALL IS THE NEW BIG: GEN Y'S ROLE IN THE RISE OF NICHE MARKETS

Small Is the New Big is the title of the bestselling book by Seth Godin. It is a fantastic book and I highly recommend it. The premise of the book is essentially that although at one time huge conglomerates dominated every market with smaller companies left to fight over the proverbial table scraps, now it is the small businesses that have the advantage.

It is a profound concept currently confronting many businesses of all sizes. It is so important that many authors have written books on the topic; for example, *The Long Tail* by Chris Anderson. The somewhat confusing title actually refers to the statistical curve that shows that the number of customers falls precipitously in relation to decreasing business size. The "long tail" is in reference to the growing significance of niche businesses in relation to overall customers.

Both are great books and worth reading; however, what both these books neglect to discuss at any length is the huge role Gen Y plays in bringing this phenomenon to fruition. The increasing significance of small fringe companies and the shrinking sales of huge conglomerate companies is in direct correlation to the beliefs and mind-set of Gen Y. In previous generations, large conglomerates were preferred over smaller unknown companies. Consumers felt they could take reassurance from a large company's reputation and were ensured a product or service of superior quality. However, by comparison Gen Y has shifted back to a

pre-industrial revolution mind-set of enjoying the work of artisans and not mass-produced, soulless products. It is important to understand the thought process and values behind this niche market revolution, in order to better explain where the trend will be headed in the future and how best to capitalize on it.

1. Why Gen Y Hates Big Companies

Gen Y hates the idea of large corporate America for many reasons. Gen Y feels that corporations are slow to adapt to developing trends, they are often stuck in the past, they value profit more than people, they don't take the same pride in their work, and they are just too common. For a small business it is important to understand these principles and to define your brand in a way that shows how you differ from your behemoth competition. As a large business it is important because all these complaints can be addressed in how you present your company to Gen Y and you can make these consumers identify with you in spite of your size. After all, no one would consider Apple to be a fringe company, and yet it has managed to enjoy the same benefits as a much smaller company.

Firstly, Gen Y feels that most big companies are slow to adapt to developing trends, and the reason they feel this way is because it is absolutely true. When gas prices were peaking in the summer of 2006, General Motors (GM) was still making the Hummer, the Corvette, and trucks so massive they had their own gravitational pull. Sure they had a few compact cars, but they were about as cool and hip as a military buzz cut. This is why I personally could not imagine going into a GM dealership for anything but directions to another car lot!

If you would like to see exactly why GM almost went bankrupt, simply go to its website and look through its line of vehicles, and try to find even a handful you would be willing to buy. Most of the cars have all the youthful appeal of an adult diaper! Whereas new small auto manufacturers such as Tesla Motors, from California, has waiting lists over a year long for its amazingly sexy full-electric sports cars. I want to have one of those cars! They are futuristic looking, fast, and fully electric. The only thing that keeps me from running out to join the huge waiting list is the high price tag, which is a result of the limited production capacity of a small producer. However, if a major manufacturer were to produce the same vehicle en masse, the price could be reduced substantially and put these amazing roadsters within most of Gen Y's price range.

Ultimately, large companies are slow to adjust, and as a result most are very out of touch with their customers' wants, especially their young Gen Y customers. Most are still catering to the wants of the Baby Boomers and just hoping Gen Y has the same needs.

Large companies are slow to adjust, and as a result most are very out of touch with their customers' wants, especially their young Gen Y customers.

2. Big Companies Are Stuck in the Past

The next big Gen Y complaint is that big companies are stuck in the past. General Motors (GM) once again embodies this principle well; it came up with the Corvette in 1953 and now, more than 50 years later, it is still the company's premier sports car. The company had over half a century to come up with something new and it couldn't pull it off.

However, GM is not the only offender. Most large businesses' core business model is obviously many decades old, with innovations added ornamentally to the outdated model, instead of actually incorporating and changing the structure. Much like putting a hat on a cow and claiming it is now something else, at the end of the day it is still just a cow. It feels equally absurd when a big company does just that with its marketing in an attempt to appeal to Gen Y. For example, at one point Washington Mutual decided to change its name to WaMu. It is this kind of shallow attempt of being new and different without actually changing anything that feels embarrassing and silly; it's like listening to your parents trying to use new slang!

3. Profits over People

Another issue Gen Y has with large corporations is that we think they value profit over people. Gen Y's beliefs come from growing up in a world where seemingly everyday on the news a large company is conducting massive layoffs of lifelong employees to balance its books. Also, stories of companies using sweatshop labor in foreign nations to help reduce production costs, or outsourcing thousands of jobs to India to save on salaries. There has been ample evidence throughout Gen Y's life to believe that large corporate titans worship only one thing: the almighty dollar and they will step over anyone to get it. As you can imagine, this does not fare well in the minds of Gen Y.

I have even been chastised on many occasions for shopping at Walmart. My Gen Y friends would say, "They don't pay their employees a fair wage, and they sell products made from unethical foreign labor, you shouldn't ever shop there. You are just making it worse." To which I respond, "It is 4:00 a.m., and I need milk, eggs, duct tape, scissors, a new lightbulb, dog food, and a quart of motor oil. Do you have a better idea? I will be twice as ethical tomorrow to make it up to the world!"

By comparison, Gen Y is almost irrationally loyal to companies they believe value people over profit. A sharp contrast to Walmart would be Whole Foods Market, or "Whole Paycheck Market" as I like to call it. This is a company that milks the virtuous company angle, and then calls said milk organic and sells it for $8 a gallon. I have had a lot of lectures from my fellow Gen Ys on the benefits of shopping at Whole Foods Market. "They pay their employees better and give them good benefits, plus all their food is grown on sustainable farms, and their animals are ethically raised," is the constant argument. Which I think for three times the price of Walmart they better pay their employees better, heck give each one a Mercedes at that price! Considering that Whole Foods Market as a company was founded in 1980 and in 2007 the company was able to buy Wild Oats Market for 565 million dollars, it wouldn't be much of a stretch to say it is doing well from virtuous branding.

Furthermore, donating part of the proceeds to charity seems to be enough to extol any company to a saintly status. If a store says that a portion of sales goes to help educate children in Africa, Gen Y will shop there frequently and readily pat ourselves on the back for doing so, as though by purchasing a bagel for breakfast we were flexing our philanthropic muscle. I am always suspect of these claims because they rarely say how much of the proceeds are being donated to charity. Is it 50 percent of sales or $50? This is never mentioned and most of us don't seem to care. That is how blindly infatuated we are with altruistic-minded companies. Which makes it quite surprising that more large companies don't participate more heavily in charitable acts, or why the ones that do don't make a greater effort to show Gen Y what they are doing to help change the world for the better.

4. Quality over Quantity

Another reason Gen Y flocks to the smaller companies is because they feel large companies don't take the same pride and put the same effort into their products or services. For example, one of my female Gen Y friends only orders her makeup from a woman who makes all her products by hand. This results in many obvious shortcomings, such as having to order a new product well ahead of time and wait for the woman to make it and then send it to her, as opposed to just stopping at the local shop and buying a new tube of lipstick on the way home. Furthermore, there is a degree of inconsistency. Since each product is made by a woman and not a machine, there is a slight difference each time, this gets offset by the personalization factor, in which the consumer can request slight color or texture changes on the next order. Finally, the makeup is much more expensive, costing well over twice as much as its store-bought equivalent.

Why would my friend willingly pay twice as much and have to wait for her makeup instead of just buying L'Oréal from the local store? Because she feels the stuff she gets made is much better quality. She is right; the woman uses higher-grade ingredients than one would find in the average mainstream makeup product. It also contains no preserving agents, since it doesn't have to sit on a shelf for months at a time waiting to be purchased. This makes it easier on my friend's skin, meaning she doesn't get any blemishes as a result of her makeup. For most women this is a substantial bargain at any price.

5. Cookie-Cutter Companies

The final and probably the most important reason Gen Y doesn't like big companies is because they are just too common. This goes back to the principle discussed in the previous chapter: Gen Y loves to research and make savvy purchases. What better way to show what a smart and diligent consumer you are than to buy from some new up-and-coming company? The coveted "underground" brand is the Holy Grail in Gen Y shopping.

The final and probably the most important reason Gen Y doesn't like big companies is because they are just too common.

I often hear my friends talk of how they used to buy a brand of shoe, before the shoe became trendy. It is strange, but to hear them talk it is almost like they feel they helped contribute to their success — like the record label representative who discovered Nirvana! Most companies fail to comprehend how important this is to Gen Y consumers. We don't want to have the same shirt all our friends have; we want ours to be unique and make a statement about who we are as individuals. The basic economic principle of "scarcity breeds value" is alive and well with Gen Y.

I am no exception. I revel in the opportunity to proudly show off a shirt I bought from a small shop while in New Zealand. It is not necessarily a better shirt, as the creators are not world-renowned tailors by any means. The design on it is not anything unique in that an American graphic designer couldn't have created. What makes this shirt so impressive amongst the Gen Y community is how unique it is. Odds are no one else I know in North America will have the same New Zealand small-label shirt I have, and that alone is enough to make it cool.

Gen Y buys from fringe companies because we believe it helps define who we are. This more than any other factor is probably the number one thing driving the rise of the niche markets. It helps us express that we are unique, knowledgeable, and well informed. This principle is illustrated quite well by Gen Y's musical tastes. When I sit around with a couple of my fellow Gen Ys and we decide to compare our music collections we always focus on what we have that is rare. We would never boast having the album from a top-ten artist, who cares about them? We brush over what is common or popular and show off what we have that our friends may not have heard of. "Check out this next band, it is an unsigned British electronic punk band," a friend would preface before playing a song. Ironically, if the band is unsigned it is probably because they are not as good as the band a record label saw fit to sign and produce. It doesn't matter to Gen Y because, like my New Zealand-crafted shirt, the value is in the uniqueness of the band.

Inevitably the "long tail" will continue to expand as options become more diversified and Gen Y consumers continue to grow in prominence. For small businesses, this affords fantastic opportunities to compete successfully against juggernaut companies, unlike any other time in history. David really can slay Goliath by understanding and appealing to Gen Y consumers.

For big businesses you can learn how to reach Gen Y consumers and still connect with us on a level that we can identify with. It is ultimately not about the size of the company but the values and principles on which a company is run. Small businesses have the advantage because their values are more closely aligned to what Gen Y likes. However, it won't matter if you don't take the time to express how your company is different from the conglomerate competitors.

You must actively associate your company with the principles discussed in this chapter. Work with charitable causes, treat your employees well, be dynamic, be on the cutting edge, and take pride in your final product. Make these traits part of your company DNA, so they become who you are and how your customers see you. If you can accomplish this, you too can have irrationally loyal Gen Y customers.

six
USING CUSTOMIZED MARKETING TO APPEAL TO GEN Y'S EGO

Gen Y has grown up in a world tailor-fitted to their every need. Products were designed through focus groups and vast research to ensure they met Gen Y's wants and needs. As technology was increased companies were able to customize each product to each individual in Gen Y.

The earliest example in Gen Y's life would have to be the Cabbage Patch Kids, released in 1982, interestingly the same year the first Gen Ys were born. The secret of these rather creepy looking dolls, was that no two were the same, each one was unique and as special as the child to which it was given.

However, it did not end with Cabbage Patch Kids, quite the opposite, when other companies saw the success in the "each product being special" angle, they all sought to replicate Mattel's success. A quick look at the most popular toys of the '80s and early '90s tells the tale, toys such as My Little Pony, which had the word "my" right in its title, and the Pound Puppies that had unique names and features.

From a very early age we were trained that each of us were unique and special. Our egos were bolstered and solidified even before we could ride a bike. As a result, Gen Y now has a healthy ego, and we think quite highly of our opinions. For companies trying to market to Gen Y, this affords a great opportunity. Because we are so obsessed with our individuality, a company can easily use this principle to make any product or

Gen Y has never known a world of limited technology, so as technology increased annually by leaps and bounds so did our expectations.

service immensely more appealing to Gen Y. However, it is important to fully understand the source of this ego boom in order to fully capitalize on it.

1. The Role of Technology in Increasing Expectations

As was the case with Cabbage Patch Kids, the trend toward customization is in direct correlation with advances in technology. With Cabbage Patch Kids, the cost of manufacturing was going down in the 1980s as more companies sought inexpensive foreign manufacturing. The extra effort, or expenditure, toward creating individualized products became more feasible, or cost effective. It is not that companies before the '80s didn't want to provide customized products, it was just unfeasible. The extra cost of doing so would have put any product outside of the cost range of the average consumer. Companies simply mass-produced uniform product lines, and consumers bought them solely because they had no other choice. As Henry Ford once remarked of his famous Model T, "The customer can have it in any color he wants, as long as it's black."

Gen Y has never known a world of limited technology, so as technology increased annually by leaps and bounds so did our expectations. Nowhere is this more evident than in video games. I remember playing the regular eight-bit Nintendo back in the '80s and being thrilled to be able to enter my name into a video game and have the game incorporate my name into the written dialogue. However, only five or so years later, I couldn't imagine a game that didn't let me name my own character and pick its attributes. In fact, in something as simple as a wrestling video game, I was able to change everything about my character, such as his clothes, his name, and even his hair color. This was where I got the idea to dye my hair blue in high school; needless to say it looked better on the video game wrestler!

Fast-forward another five years, my hair was no longer making a statement, and technology had once again increased expectations. Now I was able to upload my own photo to the video game and paste it on the face of the skater I designed on *Tony Hawk's Underground*. Why would I need to see my own exact likeness in a video game dedicated to performing skateboard tricks that spit in the face of the laws of gravity? Why not? Sure it didn't make any sense, but my friends and I loved the feature, I even went out and bought the game despite the fact that I hate Tony Hawk's video games. The amount of customization these days is astounding. I have literally spent hours designing a character for a video game, and I dare say less planning went into creating me.

2. The Ultimate Technology That Has Increased Customized Expectations

Not surprisingly, the technology that has most impacted Gen Y expectations has been the proliferation of the Internet. The technology that literally put the world at our fingertips was also a world where everything was customizable.

From an early age of both Gen Y and the Internet, we got to pick our email address, and our AOL Instant Messenger screen name. Not only could we be creative and individualized with these, we pretty much had to be. If we were to select only our exact name as our screen name, we would receive a collective unenthused yawn from all our friends in school. Instead we would conceive names that were clever and expressed who we were as individuals. Names like tigerfanatic95, cookiemonster101, mr9point9, and frenchieq21 showed our individuality, albeit often quite ambiguously.

Social networking sites only exacerbated the need for customization. I remember learning how to write lines of HTML code just so I could change the background color on my MySpace page; the plain white page just didn't say enough about who I was. Moreover, members of Gen Y spend countless hours writing about every aspect of their personality. We painstakingly explain our favorite authors, musicians, heroes, and so on. Reading any of our Facebook pages gives you an idea of how much importance we grant to our individuality. Not that I believe anyone actually takes the time to actually read the average user's About Me section. A Gen Y's Facebook page is almost a miniature shrine to the person's individuality.

3. How Companies Can Use This Ego Boom to Promote to Gen Y

To a certain extent, I believe this overdeveloped ego Gen Y has is their Achilles' heel all advertisers have been searching for. There is virtually no limit to how much you can influence Gen Y consumers by appealing to their vanity. I wish I could claim to be above the fray, yet sadly I am as guilty as anyone else. I have many times paid more money for products I didn't necessarily need or want, just because I was able to customize the product.

A good example is Nike running shoes. As a rule, I don't run unless I am being chased, I go to the gym but only to lift weights, and my running and jumping is relatively kept to a minimum. However, after a friend sent me a link to the Nike "design your own shoe" website, I found myself ordering a pair of $120 shoes. The shoes have built-in shock absorbers, which would be totally wasted on me, since my normal walking doesn't produce a significant amount of shock. So why did I buy shoes I didn't need, or necessarily want? Quite simply because I got to design them. I picked the style, then I got to pick all the colors — I went with green shocks, red soles, a white top, and red accents. My friend claimed it looked like Christmas colors, but I didn't care, I was infatuated with the fruits of my creative labors. When I found out I got to write my name on the back of them, my decision was made and the shoes were purchased. Nike had successfully convinced me to pay more than three times the average amount I normally allocate for gym shoes.

I would have never ordinarily purchased these shoes, even if I had seen them in the exact color layout I picked; in a mall I would have probably passed them by. What made them so special was that I had created them, and because it was my taste and preferences that had brought them to life, they obviously had to be superior to any other shoe. After only 20 minutes designing on the Nike website I couldn't have imagined buying any other shoe.

3.1 Haunting movie trailers

Being able to customize something also works for promotional purposes. One day my sister was on her MySpace page and she found a link for an upcoming movie called *The Haunting in Connecticut*. The link said, "Haunt the movie trailer with your image." My sister, suffering from the same generational inclination to narcissism as other Gen Ys, was intrigued and clicked on the link. The trailer played and they had incorporated her MySpace profile picture into various parts of the preview. She was so thrilled by this she forwarded links to all her MySpace friends, including me.

I was also enticed by the personalized movie trailer; I made my friends who were over at my place at the time watch the trailer I was now starring in. We then repeated the process with all their profiles, and further links were forwarded to all of their friends. We weren't forwarding the link because we wanted our friends to be aware of the movie, the movie looked awful, I mean who has ever been afraid of anything involving Connecticut? We were forwarding it because a movie preview that incorporated our image was fun.

3.2 The customized watch study

A study was done with watches, in which they asked participants to assemble a watch using various components and features. The participants were asked to pick from the features and parts to assemble what they believed would be the best watch. There were hundreds of parts and features from which to pick, different faceplates, casings, bands, and so on. Each of the participants had designed a totally unique watch. Then all the watches were put on display and the participants were asked to view all of the watches and assign what they felt was a fair price for each. Every last participant priced the watch they had designed the highest. Many priced the watch they created a full 30 percent higher than the other watches. This study exemplifies that egocentrism exists within all consumers, but is heightened with the Gen Y mind-set. We believe anything we design is better, and therefore more valued than comparable products.

Gen Y does much of its purchasing from online sources.

This condition is apparent in all generations, yet nowhere is it more valuable than when trying to appeal to a Gen Y consumer. Older consumers are not necessarily as technologically inclined as Gen Y. Often they prefer to do much of their purchasing still in person whereas Gen Y does much of its purchasing from online sources. This is important because ultimately this kind of customization can only be capable in an online context. Furthermore, older generations tend to prefer simplicity in purchasing instead bountiful options. Gen Y by comparison is used to having limitless options. When one considers how we have been trained from a very early age to expect products and services to be tailored to our exact needs, it becomes clear why customization is so much more effective with Gen Y.

4. Why the iPhone Is Popular

A great example of how customizable products will excel over their competitors is the Apple iPhone. I remember when the iPhone first came out. I was admittedly intrigued, but its high price tag seemed unjustifiable to me. Then I played with my friend's iPhone. He had already customized every feature, from the background, the icons, and the name on the slide bar. You name it, he had changed it. I was astounded by the capacity of the phone; my current phone only let me set my background image and ringtone. My jealousy was so strong I immediately went out and bought one of my own.

Once again, I had been persuaded to pay far more than I would have ever imagined I would pay for a cell phone. Moreover, my previous cell phone met all my requirements. In fact, the QWERTY keyboard I had on my old phone was better than my iPhone, since the keyboard on the iPhone can prove slightly tricky when drinking as much coffee as I do! However, the temptation for customization proved too strong to resist. I still have my iPhone, and it is fully personalized to my liking. Moreover,

I would gladly pay the outrageous expense to buy a new one when I need it, unless something even more customizable comes out.

At the end of the day, Gen Y demands unique and individual products and services. All of our lives we have been convinced that we are special, ignoring the obvious fact that if all of us are special than ultimately no one is special. However, it is important for companies to understand this aspect of Gen Y's mind-set, because of the fantastic opportunities it affords them.

You can easily convince Gen Y to pay drastically more money for products we weren't even in the market for in the first place. You can get Gen Y to promote a movie we don't even think looks that good. Moreover, the publicity for personalized products doesn't end with just sending links to friends on MySpace and Facebook. In fact, the main promoting comes in the real world when the product is proudly displayed to all of our friends, piquing their interest in the product and perhaps prompting them to look into the product and buy one of their own.

As technology makes product personalization cheaper and easier to do, it would be foolish to not take advantage of this prevailing trend. After all, you can design your own watches all you want, or you can let Gen Y go online, design their own watch, and then gladly pay 30 percent more for a watch they feel is the best watch ever made.

seven
HOW TO WIN FRIENDS
AND INFLUENCE A
GENERATION OF PEOPLE

In 1936 Dale Carnegie published a book called *How to Win Friends and Influence People*. The book was an instant hit and is still one of the greatest selling self-help books ever, having sold more than 15 million copies globally. It is a fantastic and insightful book. The principles expressed almost a century ago are still applicable today, minus the references to US Presidents Taft and Roosevelt.

Moreover, the principles described can be further extrapolated to unveil clues on how companies should present themselves in order to best appeal to Gen Y. Principles such as "you can't win an argument," "if you are wrong admit it," "give a dog a good name," and "no one likes to take orders," are all timeless lessons. Although I have to admit the language often sounds like things I could hear my Grandpa saying, if you can ignore the corny 1930s diction, you can use the principles to be a virtuous company. Gen Y supports companies they believe are good and honest. Following the principles Carnegie was able to so eloquently describe in his book, you will be just that.

1. The Importance of Being Perceived as a Good Company

It is safe to say we don't hold on to too many other things from the early part of the twentieth century, with the possible exception of Thomas

Edison's lightbulb, but even that has been replaced by a low-energy counterpart that always reminds me of a vanilla ice cream cone. Why should we still listen to the words of a man from the 1930s? The reason is because what Dale Carnegie preached first and foremost was in essence to just be a nice guy. He was said to have more friends than anyone else in his time, and this was before Facebook or MySpace.

In order to reach Gen Y, it is very necessary to be perceived as a good company. Perhaps even more important it is critical to not be viewed as a bad company. You must ensure every customer interaction is a positive experience. In the past, a scorned customer was limited in the scope in which the person could strike back at the company he or she felt wronged by. However, new technology and the interconnected nature of Gen Y have drastically changed that. Now a scorned Gen Y customer can go online and potentially cost you hundreds of new customers; the ramifications increase exponentially with every additional bitter customer.

The effect of as little as 100 angry Gen Y customers can tilt the scale of an online forum from positive to negative. Especially when you consider that people usually only go on these forums to report either exemplary service or atrocious service. Unfortunately for companies, good and adequate experiences stand little to no chance of being reported to the online world. By contrast even the slightest unfavorable encounter can render negative feedback. For example, you will never see a review that says, "I had a very usual buying experience, that met all my expectations without exceeding any, and the customer service was amazingly adequate." Luckily most people don't have that much free time on their hands.

It is important to exceed your customers' expectations. The best way to do so is by employing the methods of Carnegie to become the type of company that Gen Y will rant and rave about both online and in person.

2. The Lessons of Dale Carnegie That Are Applicable to Businesses

Now admittedly Dale Carnegie was writing about how individuals can gain friends and influence people. In transposing these lessons to businesses it is safe to say we can ignore a few sections like the section on marriage and relationships with the opposite sex. Instead, we will focus on the other chapters of his book. The following lessons are more universal and thusly more useful to companies as well as individuals.

2.1 The importance of a first impression

You never get a second chance to make a first impression. This is as true for businesses as it is for people. The way your business is first perceived sets the precedent for all the following impressions. If the initial experience by the customer is a poor one, you will have to forever work harder to dig yourself out of that hole. Moreover, in a modern marketplace where consumer options are bountiful, odds are you will never get a second chance.

The risks of a poor first impression are much higher with Gen Y than any generation before it, due to the interconnected nature of their community. If Gen Y feels especially slighted by a company, they have the potential to influence hundreds of friends and even more strangers.

2.2 You can't win an argument

Of all Dale Carnegie's points, this one is probably the least intuitive and most fascinating. Carnegie states that it is in fact impossible to win an argument, because even if you are able to get the individual to concede to your point of view, the person will never embrace it as if he or she has come to the point himself or herself.

For instance, I can argue that my hometown hockey team, the Calgary Flames, is the greatest team to ever grace a rink, despite their lack of championship wins to prove my point. However, someone from Edmonton might, and most likely would, argue that the Edmonton Oilers are in fact the superior team. I would quote statistics from Calgary's star players such as Jarome Iginla or Miikka Kiprusoff, while Edmontonians would counter with Wayne Gretzky, and I would dismiss him as a current resident of Phoenix. This would go back and forth, and so long as no punches were thrown, eventually my friend may finally claim to see my point of view, if for no other reason than to shut me up. However, he won't actually feel any differently. He will still believe his team is better, and in fact he may even develop feelings of resentment for me forcing my views on him. This is ultimately the problem with trying to convince another individual to adapt your point of view. People like to feel they have made up their minds themselves, not that they were forced or coerced into a belief.

Carnegie suggests that instead of forcing someone to your view it is more effective to simply present people with the facts in such a way that they can come to your point of view on their own. Not only does this increase the level to which they will embrace the idea, but also eliminates all risk of resentment or hard feelings. After all, when executed correctly the whole thing was their idea, so why wouldn't they support it vehemently?

This is a very crucial point most marketers miss the mark on, when it comes to trying to appeal to Gen Y. This example is especially poignant in regard to Gen Y, because of their fiercely independent mind-set. We are

Instead of ignoring your company's flaws or trying to conceal them, you can confront them and begin to actually work on them.

virtually obsessed with the idea of our own free will. Our need for individuality is almost manic in its severity. Arguing with Gen Y to try to turn them to your point of view will be a depressingly uphill battle. In contrast, if we are under the illusion we are making the decision entirely of our own will, we will gladly agree.

2.3 If you are wrong, admit it

It is only natural to want to hide our flaws: We cloak our un-toned stomachs under layers of carefully chosen clothing, we put a throw rug over the wine stain on the living room floor, and we act like we understand a clever joke even if it was over our heads. It's true nobody's perfect but we would sure like everyone around to think we are. This is why it is especially hard for people to hear criticism or admit fault.

I have seen people continue an argument long after being proven wrong. For example, in 1985, Coke decided to reformulate its flagship product Coca-Cola and released New Coke, also known as Coke II. What was designed to give product sales a huge jump in fact had the exact opposite effect. Sales actually went down, and to this day New Coke is still regarded as one of the largest corporate blunders.

How did Coca-Cola reverse their poor fortune on this large-scale disaster? They admitted they were wrong, and reintroduced Coke Classic. Not only did this bring sales back from the slump caused by Coke II, it actually increased sales of Coke Classic from the levels it was at before the failed reformulation.

Instead of ignoring your company's flaws or trying to conceal them, you can confront them and begin to actually work on them. For instance, having an online forum where customers can go online and discuss all aspects of your business is a great way to get a better understanding of what your company may be lacking, or where it needs improvement.

Moreover, it is a great way to appear honest to Gen Y customers. Seeing a few poor reviews on a company's forum is not necessarily a bad thing. A Gen Y customer will weigh out what a bad review says and contrast it against more favorable responses. The important thing is that when this discussion is held on the company's own website it makes the company look very honest and forthcoming. This goes a long way in the minds of Gen Y consumers. We feel if a company is willing to give an open forum for customers to go online and review it, good or bad, the company must be more concerned with keeping the customer happy than it is with keeping its image perfect.

2.4 Give a dog a good name

"Give a dog a good name" is an example of the corny 1930s terminology that I was talking about in the beginning of this chapter. However, despite its cheesy shortcomings, this is a very good point in reaching Gen Y customers. A good name and correlating brand is essential in having Gen Y customers identify with your company and promote your brand.

No matter how good your service or product, if your name is hopelessly outdated or mundane, it is less likely to be promoted within the Gen Y community. Gen Y loves clever names like CU Latte, Florist Gump, Lord of the Fries, or Lettuce Eat. If I were to see a sign with any of these names, I would want to know more about the company, and I would be more likely to mention the clever name to my friends.

By contrast, outdated names don't earn nearly the same kind of credit. Large companies have sought to overcome this by changing or altering their name, such as Washington Mutual changing their name to WaMu; or my favorite was when Cingular changed their name back to AT&T but with the letters in small case, so at&t. Although it is clear from these examples that few businesses ever go far enough to make their name actually more intriguing to Gen Y.

One company that realized the importance of this principle was Maui Beverages company. To try to express that it was a different kind of company it went through and changed the titles of the management. CEO, which normally stands for Chief Executive Officer, was changed to Chief Entertainment Officer. The CTO, or Chief Technology Officer, become the Chief Tasting Officer. It was a drastic change, but it worked even better than anyone at the company could have predicted. The company's profits rose from six million annually to ten million and continue to grow, thanks to its revitalized image that it was able to achieve just by "giving a dog a good name."

In addition to the name it is also important to keep all branding in line with the brand the name hopes to achieve. If you are trying to appear youthful and hip, it is one thing to change your name, or have campaigns that have a Gen Y appeal, but if your advertisements are still plain and boring you won't be able to fully achieve the desired effect. The name is important but it needs to be reinforced. A good example would be Maui Beverages; to reinforce its new management titles the company hosted a party. This makes sense if you want to portray you are a fun company: What better way than to host a Hawaiian-themed party with Jimmy Buffett? The party for the change in titles makes sense: Without the reinforcement, the changes may have felt a bit shallow and would not have had the same impact on brand perception and sales.

Gen Y doesn't support companies they just like, they support companies they love.

2.5 No one likes to take orders

This is probably the least shocking of all of Dale Carnegie's revelations: Most people understand that people hate to be bossed around. Although, we tend to put aside our common sense when it comes to marketing. Constantly we hear ads that order people to buy the product. We seem to forget what we already intuitively know. However, with Gen Y's fierce sense of independence, this hiccup in intuition can be quite costly. The demand can immediately turn off Gen Y consumers from your company, so instead of opening a dialogue or intriguing them to visit your website to learn more, you are immediately putting them off.

At the end of the day, it pays to be nice. Whether you were an author and motivational speaker in the 1930s or you are a company in the present day, the rules remain the same. The reason this principle is still so valid 80 years later is they charm certain aspects of human nature. People like to be treated a certain way, and by following this fundamental principle you can be the kind of company Gen Y doesn't just like, but the kind of company they love. Which is important because Gen Y doesn't support companies they just like, they support companies they love.

As times become more and more competitive and options to Gen Y consumers continue to diversify, companies need to start establishing their brands in the minds of Gen Y consumers. This will ensure Gen Y's free promoting of your company online and within their communities. Being a quality company just isn't good enough anymore, you need to be the kind of company Gen Y can feel good about using. Carnegie's principles are just that, they are simple little tips any company can use to be more virtuous.

Carnegie talks about a farm dog as an example of the importance of being likeable. He says out of all the animals on the farm the dog is the only one who makes his living by being likeable. A cow is used for milk and eventually slaughtered for its meat. A chicken is used for its eggs and eventually is killed and sent to KFC. A lamb gives us wool and lamb chops. Only the dog is kept around, fed, and sheltered, and the only thing he is expected to do is just be cool. Marketing is similar to being on the farm because being likeable can mean the difference between the life and death of your company.

eight
REBEL WITH A CAUSE: USING CAUSE-RELATED MARKETING TO REACH GEN Y

Gen Y is fiercely altruistic. They spend more time volunteering for worthy causes than any generation before them. In fact, a study done by Cone found that 61 percent of individuals in the age range of 13 to 25 feel personally responsible for making a difference in the world. Moreover, 81 percent of those surveyed said they had done some volunteering in the last year. Most important to this book, 69 percent of them claimed that they consider a company's social and environmental commitment when deciding on a purchase. Gen Y has grown up in a world flooded with problems and views it as their responsibility to help make the world a better place.

As I traveled I was amazed to meet numerous Gen Y students who were spending their summer volunteering do things such as teaching at an orphanage in Cambodia. For anyone who has never had the pleasure of spending a summer in Southeast Asia, the temperature tends to range between stifling hot and the kind of heat that would make the devil uncomfortable. Not only are these Gen Y students willing to fly to an insanely hot developing country to help the less fortunate, they actually pay large sums of money to do so. The cost regularly exceeds $2,000 and that doesn't include airfare. Many of these summer vacation humanitarians work and save all throughout the school year in order to pay to live in very basic conditions only because they want to help the less fortunate. It certainly is a departure from earlier generations who spent their

Every company should have some social outreach program and they should publicize it incessantly.

summers getting drunk at their parents' lake house. It is clear Gen Y places high importance on humanitarian acts, so it is important for companies to take the time to understand this inclination to be philanthropic.

1. If a Tree Falls in the Woods ...

Gen Y expects so much of themselves; obviously, they would appreciate the same kind of social responsibility from the companies they support. However, most companies, especially small businesses, have no social outreach program. Moreover, of those who do, they spend very little time publicizing their efforts. Now some may make the argument that supporting a charity or cause as a way of advertising or to improve a business's public image is somehow tainting the process, and that all acts should be done solely for philanthropy. I would humbly submit, that to those it is helping, it makes no difference what the benefactor's motives are. A child in Africa, who got a mosquito net to cover his bed, will not be kept up at night worrying if the company that donated these nets to his village did so as a publicity stunt. He will just be glad to know that he will wake up in the morning safe from the fear of having contracted malaria or any other disease transmitted by mosquitoes.

I believe that every company should have some social outreach program and that they should publicize it incessantly. Very few times in business do we actually get what the game theorists would call a true win-win scenario. The company gets more business because Gen Y consumers appreciate its work to make the world a better place, and many worthy charities and causes get the funds and resources necessary to carry out their work. Furthermore, the donations made to many nonprofit organizations can be written off on the business's income taxes. When you consider all the benefits, such as free publicity, it is amazing that few companies have social outreach programs.

It is not just enough to do a good act. Gen Y has to know about it for it to achieve an advertising impact. This makes many companies uncomfortable because they view publicizing their humanitarian acts as akin to bragging, and that somehow cheapens the act. The problem is a business doesn't have the same luxury of an individual that can hope a friend might announce his or her humanitarian efforts to a group of friends at a cocktail party and the individual can then sheepishly divulge the details, nonchalantly brushing off praise. For a business, if it doesn't actively tell people about humanitarian efforts and what it has been able to achieve, how will people find out? Simply put, they won't.

2. Ford Philanthropy

I was amazed when I started researching various large companies to try and find sponsors for my own nonprofit organization, the Teach a Man to Fish Project. (See how easy shameless plugging can be, so watch your toes because I plan on dropping my organization's name a few more times before this chapter is done.) I was amazed at how much many of these large companies were already doing to support some very worthy causes. However, I had never heard about any of the causes they supported. I had to dig deep into their websites to find anything, and even then the details were scarce. I had to research it further myself to reveal what incredible acts these companies were doing.

One organization that stuck out in particular was the Ford Foundation. It doesn't just have a few programs it has a whole foundation! One cause it is heavily involved in is fighting for women's rights internationally. Another initiative being spearheaded by the Ford Foundation is expanding accessibility to quality housing. The final example I will give is expanding livelihood opportunities to low-income regions. In all, the Ford Foundation funds more than 15.6 billion dollars to different programs and causes every year. The foundation has been around for more than 70 years, and I can't even begin to imagine all the great things this organization has been able to accomplish. Yet, I had never heard of it before.

After I read about all the great things the Ford Foundation was doing I felt like running out and buying a Mustang on principle alone. This drastically affected my decision-making process when it came to buying my next vehicle, far more than any commercial I have seen from the Ford Motor Company. In fact, every time I see a Ford car now, I think of all the great things the company is doing. I can say without hyperbole it has made me fully reevaluate my feelings about Ford as a company. I even stopped making jokes that Ford is just an acronym for "Found on Road Dead," although "Fix or Repair Daily" still slips out from time to time.

3. It's Not Just about How Much Money You Spend

It is important to note you don't need massive amounts of money to fund an entire foundation in order to influence Gen Y customers. A good example is a small bar I found in the lovely beach town of Nha Trang, Vietnam. The bar is consistently packed every night of the week, seemingly for no good reason. The name of the bar is Crazy Kim Bar.

Illogical associations are the main problem with many companies' social outreach programs.

Crazy Kim's doesn't excel because of marketing. There are many other great bars on the beach, many of which are in fact nicer than Crazy Kim's, and they offer better drink deals yet they sit empty. The reason is because Kim, the owner, donates part of all her proceeds to a program that helps teach street kids to read and provides them with an education that will give them a better future. To Gen Y this makes it worth paying slightly more for each drink, because they admire the ethics of the business and that trumps the bars with nicer decor and inexpensive drinks.

4. If It's Going to Make Dollars It's Got to Make Sense

An important aspect to remember in selecting a cause to associate with is it must be relevant. Illogical associations are the main problem with many companies' social outreach programs. For example, a friend of mine runs a chain of tanning salons. Once he decided to include in one of his newsletters that part of the month's proceeds would be donated to the American Society for the Prevention of Cruelty to Animals (ASPCA).

The month came and went and as promised part of the proceeds were donated. Unfortunately, there was no significant difference in sales as a result of the campaign. The reason was because although it is a nice thought, it didn't have anything to do with his business or customer base. He had over-personalized the campaign. He chose the ASPCA because dogs were his passion. This is admirable and it is true that many people love dogs, but to truly motivate Gen Y, the act must make sense in context with the business or client base. If he instead runs a dog boarding business or a dog food company, his cause may have crystallized more in the customers' minds.

This is a good example because the association for social outreach is not very obvious for a business like a tanning salon. The main charity cause one could easily associate with a tanning salon is skin cancer, but since skin cancer may be a direct result of using tanning salons, mum is the word.

A slight ambiguity is common for most businesses when trying to establish a relevant cause to support. Often a company must look a little deeper to establish exactly what it is selling to its customers.

Let's consider our tanning salon example again. What does a tanning salon really sell to its customers? Tans? Wrong, what a tanning salon sells is self-confidence in appearance; people pay to feel better about how they look, and ultimately to increase their self-esteem. Now, we can consider who would benefit from this boost in self-esteem and confidence. One possibility is women in shelters, who are escaping abusive relationships and are trying to get back on their feet. They can get free tans to feel better about themselves and give them the necessary confidence to search for jobs and begin to move forward with their lives. Moreover, if this tanning salon were to partner with a hair salon and a clothing company they could offer women a full makeover to help build their confidence and get them back on their feet.

4.1 It has to be newsworthy

Not only does the cause have to make sense in the mind of a consumer, it has to be newsworthy. A tanning salon donating a portion of profits to the American Society for the Prevention of Cruelty to Animals (ASPCA) doesn't stand a snowball's chance in hell of making the nightly news. However, the woman's makeover campaign as just described is the kind of local, feel-good story that leaves producers and editors begging for more. Doing this good deed means that your business will be publicized all over the local media for free. Moreover, the cost of contributing to this worthy cause for the tanning salon is virtually nothing, since the cost of electricity to run a tanning bed is close to nothing.

5. Ongoing Involvement Is the Key to Success

To maximize results with Gen Y, it is important to show commitment to the cause you support. A short-lived campaign is better than nothing, but for greatest effect, it is best to have ongoing involvement with a cause. Eventually, you can become well-known for being associated with the cause you support.

This is another one of the keys to Crazy Kim's success. She has been working for many years to help educate the street kids in Nha Trang, and now she is widely known for it. It is even mentioned in a small one-paragraph blurb about Crazy Kim's in the *Lonely Planet* travel guide for the area. Now that is being exceptionally associated with a cause: The book only had a few sentences to describe her bar to visitors and it chose to talk about her humanitarian work.

There are many great examples of companies that have managed to achieve this level of association with a cause. A good example is Avon's involvement with breast cancer awareness. The program was started in 1993; the campaign uses various products with the color pink and a plethora of corporate partners. When I was living in Auckland, New Zealand, the Sky Tower, the tallest building in the southern hemisphere, was illuminated pink to build awareness for breast cancer.

Ultimately, if you want to be able to reach Gen Y, you must take an interest in what is important to them, and nothing is more paramount in the mind of Gen Y than social responsibility.

Another great example is American Express, and its 1983 campaign to restore the Statue of Liberty. During the four months of the campaign one cent of every transaction and one dollar for every new card went toward the $2 million needed to restore the American icon. According to the *IEG's Guide to Sponsorship* during that period, transactions on American Express cards went up 28 percent.

6. Give Gen Y Results They Can See

The final aspect necessary to achieve the greatest results is to be able to see progress from your efforts and to share it with your customers. The main reason the Children's Fund, formerly the Christian Children's Fund, has been so successful for more than 70 years is that it constantly updates sponsors with results in the form of pictures and letters from the actual children they are helping. This is important because it personalizes the philanthropy and puts a face to the dollar figure.

Seeing the results of the work really brings it home in the mind of the average Gen Y consumer. Pictures and videos of individuals affected are always more memorable than numbers. Such has always been the case. Thousands of facts and figures poured out of Vietnam during the war, but one thing most people can remember is the picture of the small girl running who had been covered in napalm. This characteristic of human nature is heightened in Gen Y because our attention span is shorter. In fact, it is all I can do to consistently try to remember this point when I feel compelled to check my Facebook account every ten minutes. So it is important to provide Gen Y with simple but poignant updates in order to have your humanitarian progress stick in their minds.

A company that has accomplished this exceedingly well is Kiva.org. How the charity is able to promote so much interaction from donors is that it allows donors to pick which business to which they want to grant their micro-loan. For example, I go online and get to browse hopeful business owners from various parts of the world, look over how they plan to spend my donation, and then I can keep in touch with the new business owner and get updates on how the business is doing.

Ultimately, if you want to be able to reach Gen Y, you must take an interest in what is important to them, and nothing is more paramount in the mind of Gen Y than social responsibility. We spend our summers roughing it in developing nations, we spend our weekends volunteering our time, and we even spend more money to frequent businesses we believe want to help our community and not just profit from it.

When I think of all the great Gen Y volunteers we have at Teach a Man to Fish Project (I told you I would plug it again) and how hard they work for what they believe in, I would say philanthropy is possibly the most important thing to Gen Y. To ignore this aspect of whom Gen Y is when trying to appeal to them is inexcusably shortsighted. Find a cause that is relevant to your business and begin working to help and associate your company today. Do it because you get to write it off on your taxes; do it because it will help you gain countless new Gen Y customers; but mostly do it because it is just the right thing to do and you will feel good knowing you are making a difference.

Cough! www.teachamantofishproject.com … Cough! Cough!

nine
USING THE INTERNET TO REACH GEN Y

Utilizing the Internet and the many opportunities it affords businesses has become an essential part of doing business in the twenty-first century. Your Internet presence may well be your most important presence especially when trying to sell your products to Gen Y customers.

These days almost every company, regardless of its size, knows they must have a website. Even something this basic wasn't so obvious to many large industries as recently as ten years ago. In 1999, when the movie *The Matrix* was first announced by its creators, the now famous Wachowski brothers, Internet geeks around the world flocked to www.thematrix.com. Unfortunately for the millions of fans eager for more information about the upcoming film, the website only led to a computer supply company's modest web page. The surge in visitors soon overloaded the small server. The studio had forgotten to buy the .com address for a multimillion-dollar film! The added irony was that the film was *The Matrix*, a science fiction, futuristic action film that centered around the Internet and the evolution of computers. Though as big of a mistake not getting the .com address was, it was still not the biggest mistake involving *The Matrix*. That distinction would have to go to Will Smith, who turned down the role of Neo to star in the Hollywood flop, *Wild Wild West*!

The error in the studio's judgment to not secure thematrix.com before announcing the film reflects how businesses have grown to realize

Facebook offers some great opportunities for businesses to promote themselves.

that the Internet is an essential part of promoting any product or service. However, much like the studio that produced *The Matrix*, everyday businesses both big and small lose immeasurable amounts of customers by not having a fully developed web presence. Having a website is a good start, but it is by no means enough. If there are sufficient resources pointing customers in your website's direction, it stands to answer the question, "If a tree falls in the woods and no one hears it, did it make a sound?" In the same respect if a website exists on the web and no one visits it, did it ever exist at all? Go ahead and meditate on that one for a minute before I talk about how to ensure your website doesn't fall in to an existential abyss!

1. Facebook

Facebook was started as an online equivalent to the "face books" university used to distribute to familiarize students with other students. As a result, the social networking site was at first only for university students to network with other students at the same school. As Facebook grew in popularity it was made available to all people, not just students.

Traveling around the world I have found that Gen Y tends to default on Facebook in most countries. The odds they will have a profile on other sites seems slim, but almost everyone in Gen Y, especially if they are traveling, use Facebook to keep up with international friends. Although within the United States MySpace is still the most popular social networking site by number of users, given this global preference to Facebook, I believe Facebook is the dominant social networking site.

Facebook offers some great opportunities for businesses to promote themselves. The most basic is to post links to your business's website for all your friends to see and hope that a high percentage will either check out the site, or repost your link for all their friends to see. This is a pretty inefficient way of promoting, but when you consider that the cost of doing so is absolutely nothing, the question is: Why not? However, if you were hoping for something that wasn't basically the equivalent to firing a shotgun blast into a lake and hoping to hit a fish, then Facebook can help you more accurately target an audience.

You can set up a Facebook fan page just for your website. People can then become a fan of your business's Facebook page, and it will be announced to all their friends that they became a fan of your page. It will also be shown on their page, and friends can follow the link to become fans themselves. This is where a little creativity is necessary. If your business's Facebook page is just your business's name, it is hard to imagine that many people will want to become a "fan." However, if you creatively name your Facebook page with something relevant but more appealing, you could potentially attract fans en masse.

For example, I recently met an Aussie while vacationing in Thailand. We talked at length and I found out he was a professional bull rider. Since it is virtually impossible to live in Calgary during the summer and not learn about bull riding, I know a bit about the sport. As we talked about his bull-riding career, he told me about the Facebook page his nephew had made for him. The page was only about three months old and he already had more than 50,000 fans from all over the world. Needless to say I was intrigued.

The secret to the page's success turned out to be the name. Now he could have named the site "Rod the Bull Riding Aussie," I would still have been intrigued by this title because in all the time I spent in Australia I never saw one bull, just heaps of kangaroos and the occasional wallaby. However, the average Facebook user probably wouldn't have taken much interest. Instead the name of the page was just "Rodeo." This may not seem like a huge difference but consider it from the perspective of the potential fan. You could become a fan of "Rod the Bull Riding Aussie," and you know your friends would wonder, why is he a fan of this guy he doesn't even know? By contrast, becoming a fan of "Rodeo" simply says to your friends, I like rodeos. For guys this means, "I am a tough guy who isn't afraid to jump on top of thousands of unprocessed steaks and get knocked around for eight seconds at a time." For girls it often means, "I enjoy horseback riding," or more likely "I enjoy cowboys who ride in rodeos." Ultimately, Gen Y gets to make a statement about who they are, and by doing so they will promote your business.

2. MySpace

MySpace is still the dominant social networking site in the United States by number of users. Many of the features are very similar to its counterpart Facebook. One of the biggest advantages MySpace offers businesses over Facebook is ease in targeting a demographic. With Facebook, you have to know the users' email addresses, their names, or have a mutual friend in order to add them as a friend. Moreover, you can't just look at anybody's profile on Facebook; you have to become friends first (depending on users' individual privacy settings). By contrast, all MySpace profiles are open for anyone to see, unless the user specifically changes settings to block non-friends from viewing their profiles. More important from a targeted marketing stand point, you can actually search all MySpace users and narrow down your search using age, sex, location, and so on. Being able to target a specific demographic is hugely beneficial especially when trying to reach out to only a group of people within your city. That way

One of the keys to Twitter's success is its simplicity and that many users are able to "tweet" from their cell phones or other mobile devices.

when you announce an event through a bulletin message to your MySpace community, it will be announced only to people who are close enough to actually attend.

Another advantage that MySpace holds over Facebook is its use of bulletins. Anyone can post a bulletin and the message will appear specifically on the bulletin board of all your MySpace friends. This is very useful for announcing events. Using the bulletin board you can often ensure a good turnout for free, without all the effort and hassle of flyers. The other advantage over the traditional flyer method is your MySpace friends are more likely to attend because they have already made the decision to befriend you on MySpace. This plays on an interesting psychological anomaly known as "chain of obligation." If you can get people to side with you once, they are statistically more likely to continue to support you in the future; otherwise, they have to question their earlier decision of siding with you the first time. In other words, with a flyer invitation you are still a stranger, but in a MySpace bulletin you are a "friend" making an announcement. This is especially true in regards to Gen Y, because Gen Y is a very interconnected community, and it is important to them to support their "friends." More so than in earlier generations, once Gen Y takes an interest in your business or cause they feel much more obligated to do what they can to help you succeed.

3. Twitter

Twitter is a relative newcomer to the online social networking scene. Twitter stands to revolutionize social networking by doing almost nothing revolutionary whatsoever. Essentially, Twitter is like if someone were to take only the status bar from Facebook and make it its own form of social networking. Twitter eviscerates all that is lengthy and long-winded about MySpace and Facebook and forces users to cram it all into small bite-sized blurbs. You can make announcements, but they have to be done in 140 characters or less.

Instead of friends on Twitter you have "followers," which I have always thought sounds like a euphemism for stalker. You can also stalk, or rather "follow" other users. When someone adds a message to his or her Twitter page, he or she is said to be "Tweeting." Many people will make general comments about what they are doing in the day, while others use the site to post links to various relevant stories and websites.

One of the keys to Twitter's success is its simplicity and that many users are able to "tweet" from their cell phones or other mobile devices. This means that Twitter will often get a story long before it hits any other media source. For instance, one Twitter user, Mike Wilson, "tweeted" about how his plane skidded off the runway while trying to take off from Denver. People on Twitter knew about the accident long before the traditional media.

The way businesses can use Twitter to promote themselves online is by using it as a kind of gateway. If you look at the Twitter users with a high level of followers, you will see it is usually because they often post a lot of useful and relevant links to a specific topic. To establish yourself on Twitter, you must first define your area of expertise, which would be the field you are in currently. Then you must consistently post links to stories that are important to people in the same field, or links to new sites that like-minded people would find interesting and useful. The act of doing so doesn't take very much time, but the benefits from being perceived as a valuable person to follow on Twitter can be huge. Furthermore, Gen Y has a notoriously short attention span, and the short Tweets you post on Twitter are often enough to pique their interest without boring them.

4. An Updated Blog

The term "blog" itself is enough to throw many would-be bloggers off track. It sounds like something odd, something that would be hard to understand, so people just give up preemptively. However, the term is not so intimidating when you stop to understand its roots. The term "blog" is actually derived from the phrase "web log," which means an online journal. Initially, blogs were just a way for technologically savvy individuals to keep a journal that their friends could go online and read. However, as more and more people began reading these online journal entries on a more consistent basis, people quickly saw the opportunity for exploitation.

These days, popular blogs, such as the Huffington Post and Daily Kos, are seen with all the validity and weight of traditional media sources like CNN, especially among the Gen Y community. Many in Gen Y get their news exclusively through blogs because they are seen as a more pure news outlet. Gen Y views traditional outlets like CNN with large amounts of skepticism because of all the corruption and money involved behind the news generator. Most of Gen Y sees blogs as honest and relatively unbiased by comparison. As a result Gen Y tends to lend more credence to things they read in a blog than more traditional media sources.

How can businesses use a blog to promote themselves online? By posting relevant links, adding opinions or commentaries on current events, and presenting new ideas others in the same industry would find useful and interesting. It is close to the same formula for building a popular Twitter account. The difference with a blog is you are not limited in

the character count or file size of what you can say. However, you should keep the entry short enough that people will be willing to take the time to actually read it.

With a blog, you have the opportunity to not only post a link, but to quantify the content, and express your feelings on the content. Obviously, this allows for a much more personalized touch, and provides your company a way to establish where it stands on issues and not just show that you are aware of them.

The important thing to remember with both a blog and a Twitter account is that you must remain diligent. These sources cannot fully help you unless you take the time to add new content on a consistent basis. If you go a month without adding anything new, regardless of how insightful your posts have been, people will eventually stop checking in for updates.

5. Surfing the Web without Wiping out

At the end of the day, it is important to have a fully developed web presence. It is great to have a shiny, fully functional website, but you have to make Gen Y consumers aware that it exists. The best way to do so is by targeting them using the social networking sites we love so much.

I don't just like my social networking sites, I need them, and they are as vital to me as my cell phone. If I can't check my Facebook profile every day, I go insane. This is the case for most Gen Y; our lives revolve around our Facebook, MySpace, Twitter, and blog accounts. If you want to reach us, these are obvious places to start. Moreover, including web links when you contact us has the added bonus of instant availability. We are not required to remember the URL, or write it down to visit it later, we can log on right then and there.

Many companies think Gen Y is an unreachable generation of consumers. In actuality, we are amazingly easy to reach, you just have to communicate to us in the correct places. Conveying your message through these channels is not only a more effective method of promoting to Gen Y consumers, but it also shows average Gen Y consumers that your company understands them. You took the time to understand and integrate your company into our online world, and that alone shows you to be a more progressive company than your competitors who would rather continue to beat the proverbial dead horse of traditional media. Don't do what the Wachowski brothers did, when they were behind the technological curve and missed out on millions in free advertising by not having the .com address.

ten
USER-GENERATED ADVERTISING: GETTING GEN Y TO ADVERTISE FOR YOU

In recent history an interesting trend has begun to emerge with user-generated content. Technology has unlocked the next logical step from focus groups and targeted surveys. Instead of utilizing data gathered from focus groups and surveys then trying to accurately interpret the results to formulate a campaign that will appeal to a targeted demographic, user-generated content has enabled companies to cut out the third party and all the interpretation. The demographic designs the ads and products themselves. This is a beautifully simple and effective model. After all, who would know better how to appeal to the demographic than members of that demographic?

The user-generated content revolution has been seeded and proliferated almost entirely by Gen Y. This is good news for companies trying to reach Gen Y, because instead of investing exhaustive amounts of time and research trying to discover what Gen Y likes and how to promote it, companies now have the option to simply ask Gen Y and let them develop the products and market them to everyone within the online social community.

Perhaps the biggest advantage to this new system is the cost because Gen Y will actually do all this development and promotion for free. In fact, studies have shown that trying to pay Gen Y for developing or promoting products is paradoxically demotivating. To understand how to get Gen Y to develop and promote your products for free, you must first understand why Gen Y is so enthralled with creating content to publish online.

1. The Root of the User-Generated Generation

The user-generated phenomenon that is growing in significance is actually a by-product of the interactive nature of the Internet coupled with the creative and egotistical mind-set of Gen Y. From an early age we were coddled with our every creation being extolled as though it were a genuine Picasso. Gen Y's very supportive parents took an acute interest in their children's lives from an early age. We were encouraged and congratulated often. As a result, Gen Y became more self-confident. This is important to remember, because in order for a person to be willing to "publish" one of his or her creations for the world to judge, that person must have a large amount of self-confidence to think anything he or she creates is great and people will love it. Moreover, the person must believe that what he or she can create will be superior to similar creations and makes him or her deserving of fame. This mind-set that Gen Y possesses is a crucial element in the development and proliferation of user-generated content, because without it most of Gen Y would be too bashful or modest to put forth creations for the world at large to judge, often quite critically.

The second feature that caused user-generated content to explode in popularity is Gen Y's need for fame. Andy Warhol once remarked that in the future everyone would be famous for at least 15 minutes, and gauging the talent of the average reality show star, the bar has admittedly been lowered. Seemingly everyone can be famous these days, especially through the eyes of Gen Y. They grew up in a world of reality TV where average people on webcams become international sensations often, quite literally, overnight. To Gen Y, the concept of fame seems not only obtainable but also remarkably feasible. As a result most of Gen Y expects they will be famous, or at the very least would like to become famous.

The final Gen Y attribute that has fueled the user-generated content fire was the desire to be part of a community. This feature is really a result of the first two features combined. Gen Y's high self-esteem and need for fame can only lead to one logical conclusion: the need for public adulation. As a member of Gen Y, I can attest we rarely do anything just for the sake of doing it. If we write, we do so in public, such as in coffee shops, and proudly announce ourselves as writers. I am sure if Starbucks would let us, each shop would be filled with Gen Y artists painting pictures on an easel. Once done, we would proudly post pictures of our paintings on our Facebook pages for people to leave comments complimenting our creations.

The respect of others in the community is as satisfying as the act of creating. Therefore, it is vital that Gen Y be able to have their creations rated or available for comment if a user-generated content site is to be successful.

2. Why Money Does Not Motivate User-Generated Content

To a certain **extent offering** low sums of **reimbursement** actually discourages Gen Y from creating user-generated content.

When one considers all the features that motivate Gen Y to create and publish user-generated content, it becomes clear why money doesn't encourage them. To a certain extent offering low sums of reimbursement actually discourages Gen Y from creating user-generated content. This is because it cheapens the work and makes the content creators feel like petty employees and not like the artists they see themselves as being.

This is not to say that all monetary options are not worth considering. Obviously money can always have a motivating effect; it simply must be rewarded correctly in order to maximize motivation amongst Gen Y content creators. If you are going to offer money, it needs to be a more substantial sum, usually compensatory with the level of the campaign. For example, the T-shirt company Threadless.com offers the highest rated shirt designer a cash reward of $1,500. Not a bad chunk of change, but still not enough money to justify one of those huge novelty checks and balloons. Whereas when Doritos offered to let online users design its Super Bowl commercial, the grand prize was $1 million dollars. This makes sense because when the ad time Doritos is filling costs $1.3 million dollars, throwing the designer of the commercial just over $1,000 is the kind of stinginess that would make Ebenezer Scrooge feel guilty.

The important thing to note with both of these sums is they are high enough compensation to feel like a grand prize and not like an hourly wage. Gen Y is definitely okay with creating content to win a prize that ultimately is the highest form of adulation. However, creating content for a couple measly bucks makes Gen Y feel used.

3. What Makes a Successful User-Generated Campaign?

One of my favorite companies that continuously uses Gen Y-created content is Threadless.com. In fact, that in essence is the cornerstone of its business model. Threadless.com is an online t-shirt retailer. The main difference between it and other retailers is that 100 percent of the product design is user generated. The company managed to create an online environment that so aptly nurtures all the reasons Gen Y goes though the trouble of creating and publishing their creations online.

Firstly, every designer creates a profile where they can post their picture, write a bio about themselves, and the designers' profiles have links to all the shirts they designed for the site. This accomplishes the need for community, because it puts faces to screen names, and humanizes the products. This also affords individual designers the chance to achieve fame: As they continually post their creations, people might eventually become fans of their work collectively and check in specifically to see their latest work. Finally, the site offers a $1,500 reward to the top-rated designers. The site also has a rating system, which fuels Gen Y interest because it is a chance to receive numerical praise from the community. It also encourages designers to get their friends to go to the site to vote for them.

The outcome for Threadless.com is they have all their products designed virtually for free, and their website is promoted by designers for free. After all, the first thing anyone would do after publishing their creation on Threadless.com is try to get every person they ever met to go online and vote for their work.

4. The Ultimate User-Generated Site: YouTube

Though as clever of a system as Threadless.com has in motivating Gen Y to design and promote its products, the original and still greatest in user-generated content website would have to be YouTube.

YouTube was founded in 2005. Initially the idea was started after three PayPal employees were having trouble sharing a video that had been shot at one of their houses during a dinner party. YouTube has become a behemoth of modern-age media distribution. The website was bought by Google in late 2006 for a dizzying 1.65 billion dollars.

In a way, YouTube is the foundation on which all other user-generated sites are built. The ideas, which were new and innovative at the time, have become the standard. In fact, many small user-generated competitions still use YouTube to host their online content. YouTube, more than any other media source, has the ability to bring any person or business from total obscurity to fame in a matter of hours. Names like Super Obama Girl, Chris Crocker ("Leave Britney alone" guy), Laughing Baby, Sneezing Panda, and more are burned into all of our minds, solely due to their appearance on YouTube.

The secret to success on YouTube is to be outrageous and yet still relevant. When you look at sensations like Chris Crocker and Super Obama Girl, they both put an interesting spin on existing stories in the news. For Gen Y, YouTube has come to embody a media source that will express commonly discussed issues in an honest and unique manner while unconcerned with stepping on people's metaphorical toes. This is a good lesson that should be at the heart of any user-generated campaign directed at Gen Y. Only campaigns or websites that allow Gen Y to be outrageous and unique will truly reach a tipping point. There is no room for the unoriginal or the mundane.

5. What Makes a User-Generated Campaign Sink?

The number one factor that will kill any user-generated campaign before it can get started is if it is too stifling or restrictive. It is important to remember that Gen Y is doing all the designing and promoting in order to promote their own unique creations and for the chance at fame. If your campaign or site cannot offer them that, then there is no need to even bother with it.

Moreover, if a campaign is too self-serving, it will have trouble ever gaining traction. For instance, if you hold an online competition to design your Super Bowl commercial, you can't expect the designers to hit all the points you would like to express about your product. Don't even expect the most popular submission to make much sense. Remember the main publicity comes from people directing friends to your website to vote for their submission and not the strength of the final product. Placing too many initial restrictions on content will smother Gen Y interest and the only thing it will generate is a marketing flop.

6. The Ultimate Key to User-Generated Success Is Longevity

If you look at successful user-generated companies, you will note that one of the keys to their success is their ability to establish a community mindset that ensures Gen Y keeps submitting new content. Since the desire for community adulation is one of the primary motivations for Gen Y creating and promoting online content, it only makes sense to give them an environment where they can continue submitting new works.

A strange phenomenon happens when companies can successfully accomplish return-content submissions, Gen Y will come to truly identify with a company and take a real interest and pride in its success. This is the Holy Grail for user-generated companies, because Gen Y are

Since the desire for community adulation is one of the primary motivations for Gen Y creating and promoting online content, it only makes sense to give them an environment where they can continue submitting new works.

fiercely loyal consumers to companies they believe in. They will not only promote your company by asking all their friends to go online and vote to raise their creation's rating, they will insist friends use your company simply because they now feel a vested interest in your success. Given the extreme interconnected nature of Gen Y, this is a huge benefit to any company that is surprisingly easy to achieve, just give Gen Y an opportunity to express their creativity, receive adulation, and join a community. If you can accomplish these three things and hold Gen Y's interest, you can anticipate the same levels of success that Threadless.com was able to achieve. They began as a start-up company in 2000 and are grossing more than $30 million dollars just eight years later; and even opened their first retail store in Chicago in 2008.

At the end of the day, the Internet has not only made it possible to interact with Gen Y customers, but thanks to the rise in user-generated products, it has become a necessity. It represents the future of product development and promotion. It is by far the most efficient method of producing and promoting a product. It is the most simple solution that is usually the correct one. Nothing could be simpler than having the customer design the product he or she wants to buy and promote it to all his or her friends.

Every year, design software becomes more and more user friendly. I don't fancy myself a graphic designer, but even I have been able to use online design programs to create some pretty impressive websites and PDF flyers. In the next few years, technology will continue to advance to meet the needs and satisfy Gen Y's desire to create and publish content online. As a result the trend toward user-generated content promises only to intensify. Perhaps Andy Warhol's vision has yet to be fully realized. Perhaps in the future (thanks to user-generated content) everyone, for better or worse, will be famous for 15 minutes.

eleven
USING VIDEO GAMES TO ADVERTISE TO GEN Y

When Nintendo launched its first eight-bit video game console in the late 1980s, the first of Gen Y was just entering their school years. I personally remember playing my first video game at the age of five, and ever since that fateful day, I have considered the *Mario Brothers* closer than family!

The evolution of home video games coincides almost eerily with the aging of Gen Y. The first game systems were released in the 1980s, such as Nintendo and Sega Genesis. The games on these systems were relatively tame, childish even. For example, in *Mario Brothers* a person would help a pair of Italian plumbers find a princess, in *Paperboy* the player would help a paperboy deliver newspapers, and in *Sonic the Hedgehog* the player would navigate a hyperactive hedgehog through an imaginary world. These games were very obviously directed at players ten years old or younger.

Fast forward to the late 1990s. Clearly, with names like *Duke Nukem*, *Doom*, and *Mortal Kombat*, the main objective was no longer delivering the Sunday newspaper! Gen Y had grown up and demanded games of a more "mature" nature. I remember in the late 90s my friends and I would rent games solely based on how violent and gory they were, and video game developers delivered in spades.

Now, in the present, the most popular games have become games of strategy instead of mindless gore such as *Warcraft*, *Final Fantasy*,

One of the best ways to reach Gen Y that has only recently been made possible by advances in technology is ad placement in the actual video games.

and *Command & Conquer*. Gen Y has grown from violent-game-playing-addicted teenagers to 20-somethings who want to be intellectually challenged.

According to EA games, the highest purchasing group of video games is between the ages of 16 and 26. Video game companies realized long ago how important Gen Y is to their bottom line so they have worked very hard to stay in sync with this generation. As a genre that has grown from obscurity in the 80s to profiting in the current recession from Gen Ys, it would make sense to capitalize on all the video game companies' research to best reach Gen Y.

1. Ad Placement in Video Games

One of the best ways to reach Gen Y that has only recently been made possible by advances in technology is ad placement in the actual video games. Anyone who has seen a new video game knows how real they look; for example, systems such as Xbox 360 and PS3 are in High Definition (HD). Since 67 percent of the game systems sold are these two HD systems and, according to TG Daily, less than 28 percent of television viewers have an HD TV signal; therefore, ads placed in video game billboards are actually much more likely to be clearly seen on a TV than those in real sports arenas. According to the *Washington Post*, the cost of a billboard ad in the stadium where the Washington Redskins play can run from $350,000 to $500,000 a year. Now compare that to the one-time $44,000 President Obama paid during his campaign for presidency to be advertised in the new *Burnout Paradise* video game. Aside from the obvious money saving benefits, video game billboards have several more distinct advantages.

A study by Gen Y Consulting has shown that a person playing a video game is focused on the screen 96 percent of the time he or she is playing. By contrast, a person watching a football game is only fully engaged with the TV 65 percent of the game. The reason is people tend to get distracted during boring parts of the game and focus only during pivotal plays. Yet, a person playing a football video game is constantly engaged, as he or she is either picking the next play or executing it. The person would never think to go to the kitchen for another beer during a play, because every moment of the game is dependent on the player.

Furthermore, a billboard placed in a football arena will only been seen one day a week. Not many people are watching Sunday's football game over again every day of the week, or at least one would hope nobody's life would be that sad and empty! By contrast, many video game players play a video game at least once a day, and many play the same game multiple times in a single day. This means the same ad will be seen over and over again, which has huge ramifications on retention of the ad's message. In the same way, many of us can remember a funny TV commercial but can't remember what product the commercial was promoting. Repetition is crucial for memorization, especially for Gen Y. We are easily distracted and video games are one of the few things we are focused on for long periods of time.

Another great advantage for companies advertising in video games is that the practice of advertising in video games is still very new. It wasn't even possible in any real capacity until quite recently. As a result, is hasn't been over-exploited and is not yet considered ubiquitous and obnoxious.

When I see a billboard ad for a company in my favorite racing video game, I don't think "just drop dead already and leave me alone." I actually appreciate the company making my game feel that much more realistic. Plus, it feels like the company took time to market to me on my terms. Interrupting me every two downs during a real football game is not cool, it's just annoying. However, seeing an ad for a real company in my football game is exciting because all video game players crave more "realistic" games. We want the players on the field to look like the actual players, we want the crowd to look real, and we love when the stadium looks real as well. Sponsored ads make the stadium look real, so now you are giving me ads when I want them not just interrupting me when I am trying to watch a game on TV.

That is a huge difference in mind-set, one that many advertisers forget when it comes to Gen Y. Gen Y will extol and raise up a company they like, and shun one they don't. Advertise to me when I want to see your ad and I will appreciate your innovative marketing, and think your company is one I would like to support. Adversely, a company that goes the extra mile to interrupt me will earn my disdain, not my loyalty. For example, I was watching TV and suddenly a commercial came on that was much louder than the TV show I had been watching, and the ad repeated its simple pitch over and over again with the announcer actually shouting the message. I know he yelled the message because most people don't pay attention to commercials, and loud noises get attention. Also, I understand that the repetition was supposed to ensure memorization of the commercial's message. As the commercial creators predicted, it worked because the ad did get my attention, and I did remember the company and what it sold. The problem is I also committed one more fact to memory at that moment, "Never, ever buy anything from those jerks!" The company could be selling water in the Gobi desert and I would sooner succumb to dehydration than give that company one cent of my money. Despite what others may say, there is such a thing as bad publicity when it comes to Gen Y.

2. Digital Product Placement

Even more powerful than placing an ad in a video game is digital product placement. Billboard ads in video games are great because they make the game seem more realistic, and are viewed more frequently and appreciatively by Gen Y consumers.

Product placement is taking all the benefits of "in game" ads to the next level, no pun intended. Players still embrace the products in the spirit of added realism, while at the same time they can interact with the product. It amazes me how many people overlook how profound this is. This gives companies a chance to actively show consumers the advantages of their products. For example, I can drive your newest car, and actually feel the extra horsepower and better handling without ever stepping foot in the actual car. I can check out all the new features of your cell phone, laptop, or camera without ever leaving my house. You can establish value for your product; if my character saves up to buy your latest and greatest product, I will automatically associate that product as having a greater worth than a product that I got as a free sample in real life.

In 2006, 12 of the top 20 PC games were suitable for product placement, as were 14 of the top 20 console games. Yet, many advertisers have failed to see the blatant opportunity for product placement. Consider how the movie *E.T.* affected the sales of Reese's Pieces. Before *E.T.: The Extra-Terrestrial,* Reese's Pieces were a relatively unknown candy; in fact, the opportunity was first offered to M&Ms, who turned it down. After the movie's release, profits for Reese's Pieces went up by more than 65 percent. Moreover, *E.T.* was only a movie, which didn't highlight the benefits of the candy, or allow the audience to interact with it. The potential for product placement in video games is exponentially higher because of these added benefits.

One company to already capitalize on this new trend is Sony Ericsson with the use of its new cell phone in the video game *Syphon Filter*. Players used the phone and its many features to accomplish their mission. When I went out and bought that phone I felt as though I already owned it and trusted it. After all, if I trusted it to help me in covert missions of virtual life or death, I knew I could trust it to text message my friends.

Other games like *The Sims* could employ any number of product placements. The game is a sort of virtual reality, where you build your character's life. You buy TVs, computers, appliances, and all the other things used in day-to-day life. Your character goes to restaurants and buys food at the store. Basically all the things we do in real life are encompassed in this type of virtual reality game. I am astounded when I see many of the products the characters buy are generic, bearing fake names made up for these types of video games. A player must save up and buy a better TV for his or her character's swanky new apartment, and the TV he or she buys is just called "plasma TV," not Sony, Philips, or LG.

Burger King has proven that product placement doesn't have to be so obvious. "The King," Burger King's large plastic-headed spokesperson appears in many video games. He is not always relevant, but he is always hilarious. For instance, in *Fight Night Round 3* you can select "The King" as your corner guy. Does it make any sense? Not at all, but watching my boxer walk to the ring while "The King" gets the crowd all worked up for me makes me select him every time. Plus, having him in my corner helps my stats by giving my fighter more heart points, which makes my fighter more likely to get up after getting knocked down. Burger King was able to express an advantage to the gamer. Albeit perhaps not the best message when one considers the amount of heart disease that comes from fast food!

In fact, Burger King has embraced the medium of video games many times to great benefit. Burger King even released its own mini-games that came free with a meal purchase. The games were not very elaborate, just silly little games that involved "The King." However, as soon as I heard "free game," I went immediately to Burger King and bought a meal to get the game. I played the games a few times before I got bored of them, but I showed the games to all my gamer friends. I didn't show them because they were great games; they were actually pretty boring, but they were novel and funny. As a result of the free Burger King mini-games, the company saw a profit increase of more than 40 percent in one quarter.

3. Designing a Video Game to Promote a Product

Other companies have gone the extra mile and designed their own video games to highlight the benefit of their product. To promote Chrysler's new Jeep Rubicon, the company developed *Jeep 4x4: Trail of Life*. The game was free to download online, and users needed only to enter a valid email address. More than 380,000 users downloaded the free game and 14 percent of the first orders for the actual Jeep came from email addresses that had been collected to download the game. In fact, first year sales of the Jeep Rubicon were 300 percent more than Chrysler had anticipated. Perhaps if it had continued pursuing ambitious new marketing campaigns like the Jeep video game, the company would not be filing for bankruptcy.

Another American car company that hit a gold mine through developing an online game was Chevy. Chevy introduced a small online street racing game centered on its Cobalt. What Chevy did that was unique was to use feedback from users in the development of the vehicle and its accessories. It is no big secret that American cars have fallen behind in

These companies used video games to show Gen Y consumers what their products stand for, not just tell them in flashy words what they are supposed to mean.

the genre of compact street sports cars, or street tuners. The genre has taken on a life of its own in recent years, most predominantly with Gen Y consumers, who want fast customizable vehicles that are fuel efficient and inexpensive. The street tuner phenomenon has grown so large that it has sparked countless video games such as the *Need for Speed* series, and a vast number of mainstream films like *The Fast and the Furious* franchise.

If you are curious how well American cars are holding up in this new fad watch any of *The Fast and the Furious* movies: The only American car you ever see is from the 1960s. The main manufacturers to excel in this new category are Honda, Toyota, and Nissan, which might explain why these three companies have been increasing profits as the domestic market fails. In fact, in 2008 Toyota overtook GM as the largest producer of cars, for the first time in history, thanks in no small part to being able to effectively monopolize the Gen Y consumer market. In response, Chevy developed an online video game in which gamers could "customize" a Chevy Cobalt and race other cars on a simulated street track. This was a brilliant move to establish in the mind of Gen Y consumers that this domestic car could be a great tuner car, at a lower price tag than the most popular street tuner, the Honda Civic. Moreover, Chevy collected all the data from users selections on spoilers, hoods, and wheels; then it used the most popular selections and made them selections on the new Cobalt. With cutting edge thinking like that, there may be hope for domestic auto companies yet.

What both Chevy and Chrysler realized was that online video games could be a powerful marketing tool. The best magazine ad can't begin to compare with the feeling of actually winning a virtual race with a car you are considering purchasing. What would make you think a car is fast: An advertised horsepower rating, or the feeling of blowing the doors off your opponent in a virtual race? Moreover, what better way to solidify in the minds of consumers that the new Jeep means adventure than having them take it for a virtual test-drive through the Mayan jungle? These companies used video games to show Gen Y consumers what their products stand for, not just tell them in flashy words what they are supposed to mean.

At the end of the day, the options for profiting from this constantly expanding and developing medium are endless. Companies can offer test drives of their newest cars in exotic destinations, all from the comfort of the buyer's own home, with no pushy salesperson to ruin the experience. That is ultimately what Gen Y wants from a buying experience. We want you to give us all the information and let us make the decision ourselves.

We hate overly polished campaigns that try to convince us something is true when we know it isn't. Empty promises and run-of-the-mill products won't do for us. Video games enable companies to interact with Gen Y and show us firsthand why their company is better. They can show us what great products they have by letting us use them in a virtual world.

Video games don't always have to show the exact benefits of a product. After all, not all products lend themselves so seamlessly to a video game as a car. Sometimes a video game can be abstract but still help associate your brand with fun and enjoyment. One such product where the benefits would be hard to express through an interactive video game is breakfast cereal. Sure they are fun, we all enjoy the small toys that come with the cereal, but the problem is you only get the small toy after you have already made your purchase. How can you reward consumers and make them feel good about your brand even before they go to the store to make their selection? Froot Loops came up with a creative series of online games called *The Ultimate Fruity Adventure*. The objectives of the games are pretty simple — navigate simple maps and find treasure. They are not great games, and the toys have never been top shelf, yet the small amount of joy they bring has influenced more breakfast decisions than any Toucan Sam mascot could ever hope to.

4. Sponsored Video Games

A new and interesting trend that is just now beginning to emerge is the concept of sponsored video games. The same way TV and radio programs have been provided for free thanks to advertiser dollars, companies are now working to develop full-length top-quality video games that consumers will be able to have for free, thanks to advertisers footing the bill for development. This is an interesting concept because most consumers forget that they get certain radio and TV channels for free because of the commercials. Commercials are hated, and something to be avoided if at all possible, because no one feels grateful to the sponsors for bringing them their favorite shows. Admittedly even I forget that shows like *The Simpsons* and *Family Guy* were both made possible by sponsors. I never think, "Thank you Brand X for providing my favorite shows." I happily TiVo past their commercials without a second thought.

The problem with TV commercials is that shows have been free for viewers for so long, we have all lost the concept of them ever having a value. This is where video games present a unique opportunity. Gamers are all used to paying top dollar for the newest game titles; the average game costs more than $60. That's a lot of cash to put out, especially

If your company can incorporate video games into your marketing plan, your advertisements can become something to be enjoyed and not endured.

when you consider the average gamer has more than 20 games in his or her collection. Now how do you think gamers would feel about getting one of these top titles for free? How do you think they would feel about the sponsor who gave them, free of charge, their new favorite game that they would have paid more than $60 for? This then plays on an interesting aspect of human nature, the feeling of indebtedness. When we are given a gift we value, we feel highly obligated to the individual who gave us the gift. This is true especially amongst Gen Y consumers, as they are very loyal to companies they feel are "good" companies. They will pay more for products from companies they identify with.

Gen Y can learn what a fun and cool company you are by playing your online games when they are bored. They can feel grateful when you sponsor their gaming habits and give them for free what they were expecting to pay large sums of money for. But most importantly by getting involved in the video game world your company can show Gen Ys that "you get them." It shows that as a company you took the time to listen and market to them in a way they can appreciate and even enjoy. After all, that is the whole point of video games: to be fun. If your company can incorporate video games into your marketing plan, your advertisements can become something to be enjoyed and not endured.

5. Money in Games

In the wildly popular game *World of Warcraft*, players from all over the world can interact with one another in a huge virtual world. Players can talk to each other, go on missions together, work as a team to accomplish tasks that would be impossible on their own, and even engage in virtual transactions. Players are able to sell items they collect and get virtual gold in exchange. They can also find gold on their fallen enemies, and through countless other methods of trade that mimic the real world. Perhaps even stranger is that the gold in *World of Warcraft*, has now taken on real world value. Sites on eBay will sell gold that can only be used in the game, for real money. Even more odd is that there are companies in China that employ people to do nothing but play *World of Warcraft* and "harvest" gold, to be sold to players online. This illustrates a new movement in the online world in which the line between virtual reality and reality is blurring.

Another example is the virtual world of *AdventureQuest* and its more than 6.5 million monthly users. Players conduct online monetary trading similar to that seen in *World of Warcraft*. Players can earn their gold, pay real money to buy it, or sign up for corporate sponsorship and get gold for free. More than 90 sponsors have already signed on to *AdventureQuest* and it continues to grow. By sponsoring the games so gamers can play their favorite video games, companies will once again reap not only the benefit of brand reconition, but they will also gain loyal Gen Y consumers.

Perhaps the next step in blurring the line that divides the real world and virtual worlds is being able to use money from the game to make purchases in real stores. Why not accept virtual money earned to get discounts purchasing items? Companies often offer huge sales to entice consumers. However, the problem with a sale is once a consumer has paid a lower price for a product it will be difficult to convince him or her to ever pay full price for it again. The overall value of the product has been compromised in the mind of the consumer, which is the conundrum of sales. Instead, what if companies allowed potential consumers to use some of their earned virtual gold to receive money off that new purchase? Now the item's value has not been compromised and the consumer has been properly motivated to purchase the item through your company and not through a competitor — a true win-win scenario.

twelve
GO GREEN TO MAKE GREEN: THE IMPORTANCE OF ECO-SUSTAINABILITY TO GEN Y

Any company trying to appeal to Gen Y consumers would seriously be remiss not to acknowledge how important eco-sustainability is to young consumers. Perhaps it is a result of our age, because we are still young, and hence we are going to have a greater vested interest in the practices that may eventually make this planet uninhabitable. I suppose some people in their 60s might not feel so concerned about the ramifications of polluting, after all, why not play down the clock and let the next generation deal with the mess? (Much like a person moving out of an apartment might feel less than compelled to clean up after his or her farewell bash.) Gen Y, however, is inheriting a planet where the resources have been plundered and polluted for profit. We feel a strong desire, responsibility even, to reverse the practices that have wreaked havoc on our ecosystems.

From an early age we were convinced of the merits of environmentalism. I remember watching the cartoon show, *Captain Planet and the Planeteers*. The show featured a group of five young global activists, "Planeteers" if you will, who were endowed with superpowers via their rings. Each member of the group had a special power covering earth, wind, fire, water, and heart. The real magic happened when their powers were combined to make Captain Planet appear.

The show featured the Planeteers battling evil polluters and working to help preserve the environment. It is important to note that the polluters were usually villainous businessmen who sought to plunder and

If you are trying to sell a product to us, it only makes sense to place a large amount of emphasis reassuring Gen Ys that you are on the side of the Planeteers and not the polluting villain.

profit off the planet. This show was first aired in 1990, when the oldest of Gen Y were turning eight, so as you can imagine, growing up being inundated with the idea that non-environmental businesspeople were evil is going to have long-term effects on our purchasing habits. The lesson to take from this is if you are trying to sell a product to us, it only makes sense to place a large amount of emphasis reassuring Gen Ys that you are on the side of the Planeteers and not the polluting villain.

1. How to be Captain Planet and Not the Evil Villain

How can your company be seen as a progressive company in the eyes of Gen Y? How can you change your day-to-day business practices in a way that is both cost effective and efficient in solidifying your company's dedication to preserving the environment? Read on to discover how.

1.1 Recycling

Most individuals are fairly familiar with the importance of recycling as a necessary component to preserving the environment. Many business owners may have a high level of dedication to recycling in their personal lives, and yet fail to bring those values to their businesses. However, often practices that are more sustainable to the environment are also more cost effective for the business. Eliminating waste in an organization can help conserve your resources and your bottom line; they need not be mutually exclusive endeavors.

Esurance and its paperless billing system is a good example of how eliminating waste can actually help save a business money every month. Esurance advertises its commitment to being green. In a recent commercial the company's cartoon spokeswoman, Erin, battles a giant robot that is cutting down trees in a beautiful forest in order to make paper for the other insurance companies' wasteful paper-billing practices. Of course, what the commercial doesn't mention is how much money Esurance saves by not mailing physical bills. A paper bill means the company needs employees to prepare and mail the bills and it would need to buy massive amounts of paper, ink, and postage in order to mail out the bills. An email system can be computer automated, eliminating the need for extra labor costs. Also, sending the bills electronically means zero overhead on the supplies necessary to prepare and mail a bill, which is a huge savings to Esurance. The end result is Esurance is able to reduce a huge portion of operating costs, and then advertise these huge savings as an example of how it is eliminating waste and being a sustainable company. It is truly a win-win scenario. The company saves money on its operating expenses, gains new eco-minded customers, and reinforces its enviro-friendliness to the public.

The greatest benefit of incorporating a recycling program in your business model is gained from showing Gen Y customers you share their values. This is where many companies still fall behind. Perhaps because it is less than vital to their own values, many businesses only make subtle suggestions in their advertising about their recycling efforts. Often one must venture deep into a company's website to find any information on steps they have taken to be more sustainable. Unfortunately, the average Gen Y consumers are not going to search tirelessly through your site to find this information. The result is they will never learn of your recycling programs. Therefore, it is important for companies to place these programs front and center, make them brutally apparent, and impossible to ignore.

Ideas like reusable bags are an obvious way to show your commitment to recycling. However, a small unreadable notation on a product that it is made from recycled material is insufficient. If you are going to print your recycling message on a product, make it legible; in fact, make it huge! Gen Y loves to carry a product that expresses their commitment to sustainability. Moreover, products that seem to be obviously made from recycled materials often fare very well amongst Gen Y consumers.

Many of my female Gen Y friends have handbags and shoes made from various recycled material. One example, that is a huge fashion craze in Taiwan, is a shoe made from recycled newspapers. No, that is not a typo! People are actually lining up to buy shoes made out of old newspapers. The concept sounds like the kind of thing a bored five-year-old might do as a lark, but at $150 a pair these shoes are no joke. The shoes are lined with cotton for comfort and covered with a clear plastic coat to make them more durable and waterproof and glued to rubber soles. The creator, Colin Lin, says she likes that all the publicity pushes competing companies to consider creative ways they can become more eco-friendly. Not only are Gen Y consumers willing to carry something that is constructed from an unrelated item, they will pay a huge premium to do so if it is considered environmentally friendly.

1.2 Minding your carbon footprint

Thanks to the vast amount of information surrounding the consequences of global warming, carbon footprints have become a huge buzzword with Gen Y. We may see the need for recycling, in order to increase sustainability and availability of natural resources, but the consequences of carbon emissions seem substantially more grim. The idea of the polar ice caps fully melting and flooding the planet is admittedly much more haunting, and brings to mind images from the movie *Waterworld*. This is an issue very near and dear to the hearts of Gen Y.

Any company hoping to fully pull on the environmental heartstrings of Gen Y would do well to focus on carbon emissions. Understandably though, most companies don't have coal burning smoke stacks in their front yard that they can curtail to show progress, so companies must consider less obvious ways to affect the carbon footprint. One great resource for understanding and measuring your carbon footprint is the website climatecrisis.net.

The following are some tips for reducing your company's carbon footprint:

- Use compact fluorescent lightbulbs.

- Turn down the office thermostat during the winter and encourage staff to wear more sweaters.

- Turn up the office thermostat in the summer to reduce air conditioning usage.

- Replace or clean the furnace filter and air conditioner every two months.

- Buy energy efficient appliances when replacing old appliances in your business.

- Wrap the water heater in an insulation blanket.

- Reduce hot water use.

- Turn off and/or unplug electronic devices when they are not being used in the office.

- Insulate and weatherize your business.

- Implement recycling programs in your place of business for employees and customers.

- Use recycled paper products.

- Plant trees around your business, if possible.

- Switch to green power.

- Buy locally grown and produced foods at farmers' markets; buy fresh foods instead of frozen, and use organic foods if you are in a business that sells or provides food for your clients and customers.

- Stay away from heavily packaged products.

Much like recycling, for your company to enjoy the full benefit of reducing your carbon footprint, you must make Gen Y aware of your efforts. Tell Gen Y all the ways you have reduced your own business's emissions. It is also a good idea to give them an idea of how much that has helped the cause, and put it in terms that are easy to understand.

For example, a company can say on its website, "We were able to reduce our carbon footprint — an equivalent to taking 100 cars off the road. Click here to find out how." This is not an overwhelming inundation of information, and it is not confusing, but it gets the point across. Moreover, the company gets points for Gen Y customers being able to click through and see exactly what the company has done to reduce its carbon footprint, such as switching all lightbulbs to low-energy bulbs, installing energy efficient glass, or installing solar panels. Gen Y appreciates that level of transparency in companies and will reward any business that does so with fanatical loyalty.

An added bonus for companies are the many tax benefits for those who commit to reducing their carbon footprint. Gen Y is not the only one who sees the value in reducing carbon emissions. Fortunately for businesses, Uncle Sam feels much the same way. As a result, there are countless tax credits available to businesses and individuals who opt to go green.

In summation, a company reducing its carbon footprint gets more Gen Y customers, lowered bills, tax incentives, and the sense of doing the right thing in order to help make this world liveable for generations to come.

A company reducing its carbon footprint gets more Gen Y customers, lowered bills, tax incentives, and the sense of doing the right thing in order to help make this world liveable for generations to come.

2. Show Your Support to Eco-Sustainability

To further show commitment to the environment, companies can choose to support or work on issues that are larger than their company and their exact impact. Large conglomerates and their outdated policies of cutting corners to increase profits at any cost are perpetrating many of the issues that are drastically impacting the planet. For example, clear cutting the rain forests to get to the fertile soil that sustains the rain forest. Some companies love to use the soil from rain forests because it is full of nutrients and results in huge crops and bigger and faster profits. Moreover, much of this land is bought inexpensively through unethical partnerships with the ruling parties in some of these developing nations.

The problem is that the fertile soil that is the foundation for the entire rain forest is not very deep. Therefore, when the forest and ecosystem needed to replenish the soil is removed, the land becomes barren and unusable after only a few growth cycles. It is chilling to see a vast area of arid land that used to be a bustling, self-sustaining rain forest and home to millions of creatures just so some company could grow a few cycles of a cash crop. It is unfortunate that this is one of the biggest problems facing the environment, especially when one considers that the trees being clear-cut used to be removing excess carbon dioxide from the atmosphere; this in turn accelerates global warming.

Though there is hope, even when smaller companies are not responsible for such offensive business practices, they have the power to choose to not work with these companies. This is a great way for companies to show Gen Y consumers the depth of their commitment to eco-sustainability, and it is not very taxing on the company. A company can just make it known on its website that it does not buy from any supplier who uses practices that are unethical. One company that has done this very thing to great success is Trader Joe's.

Trader Joe's has a strict policy of being environmentally conscious themselves and expecting the same from all their suppliers. In fact, in one example, Trader Joe's stopped buying eggs from a provider called Gemperle. An infiltrating member of Mercy for Animals made a video of internal animal abuse that routinely occurred. As a result, Trader Joe's stopped carrying the product. It is this kind of ethics that make me and many of my Gen Y friends love Trader Joe's. We go buy items from Trader Joe's with a clear conscience because we can trust that Trader Joe's carries products that are ethical and from other good companies. It really is hard to overstate what a huge bonus this is for companies trying to earn the loyalty of Gen Y.

3. Organics

Organics is also a way Trader Joe's exemplifies yet another principle of Gen Y's obsession with environmentalism. The conditions behind how the raw materials were farmed have become of vital importance to Gen Y consumers. Organics have become a booming business and for a good reason, Gen Y customers really want organic products. We are willing and wanting to pay substantially more for organic products. I have known many of my Gen Y friends to complain when not given the opportunity to pay more for organics.

What is an organic product exactly? There is a surprising amount of confusion behind what being "organic" means. Essentially when something is organic it means the product is grown without the use of chemical pesticides.

However, it doesn't end with consumables. Items such as cotton, hemp, bamboo, and cork can also be organic. For example, cotton could be organic, which affords a great opportunity to go "organic" to many businesses that don't necessarily deal in food products. A clothing store can offer organic cotton jeans, or organic cotton T-shirts. Even a company that doesn't sell food- or cotton-based items can offer its customers organic, reusable shopping bags. You don't have to give them out to every customer because this would obviously become quite expensive very quickly. Having organic bags prominently available for sale will help make a statement to customers that your company "gets it" and shares the customers' values.

Ultimately though, "organic" is a big buzzword, and the very mention of it gets Gen Y all worked up, much like how a dog reacts to the word "treat." It is hugely advantageous for companies to be able to incorporate the use of organics into their business model in some capacity.

It is hugely advantageous for companies to be able to incorporate the use of organics into their business model in some capacity.

4. Buy Local

Another trend that has emerged as a result of Gen Y's push toward going green is the inclination to "buy local." This affords great opportunities to small businesses. Often, small businesses will go out of their way to appear bigger than they really are. In a way, most businesses are still stuck in the mind-set of the previous generation in which people preferred to do business with a multinational company. Constantly, small, local businesses will do things to give themselves the facade of much larger companies. For example, telling customers to call the corporate office, which inevitably leads to the company's only office that is in the founder's home a few miles down the road. Start-up businesses need to shake this outdated inclination and embrace their earnest roots, to have Gen Y embrace them.

The founding principle behind "buy local" was that buying an item which was grown in California and then loaded on to a refrigerated truck, only to be driven across the country to Florida to be sold in a grocery, is extremely wasteful. The amount of resources as well as the emissions emitted from this practice are staggering. However, if the same products are grown locally, we can reduce costs and emissions on this very wasteful practice.

People like the idea of buying local because their money is going to support farmers in their own community and not on the other side of the country. Also, if the money stays within the community, the farmers will turn around and spend their profits within the same community. The end result is that the local economy is strengthened, neighbors support their neighbors' businesses, and no one is selling each other out to save a few cents on a pound of bananas.

The idea is applicable to more than just produce, and has gained momentum in other industries as well. For instance, what could be more wasteful than manufacturing a product in the middle provinces of China, only to load it onto a truck to drive it to a port town like Beijing? Once there, the product is loaded on to a boat and sailed halfway around the world to Long Beach, California. Then it is once again loaded onto a truck and then driven across the country to New York to be sold at a chain store. By the time it is finally ready to be purchased, the product will probably have traveled more than the person buying it. I wish I could say this Rube Goldberg system (meaning to make the system more complicated than necessary) of economic supply and demand was a rare occurrence, but to the contrary the majority of items sold in North America go through this very complex system to get to their destination. It is almost hard to imagine a system that could be more wasteful than this. It is the equivalent of cooking a 30-pound turkey, then eating one wing and throwing out the rest!

Not to mention the strain this system puts on the economic future of North America in general. If one country continues to buy all its products from another country without the other country ever buying anything in return, things are unbalanced. Hence, why China is currently the biggest holder of United States debt. It's an odd thing when a communist country is the one funding unbridled capitalistic tendencies.

Buy-local initiatives seek to usher in a little sanity to this unsustainable equation. Gen Y doesn't want a future in which all jobs are sourced to foreign countries in order to save a few dollars. We are willing to spend a little more money if we know the product we are buying is produced locally. It just makes more sense; that way the money can stay in the community and can be spent to help other local businesses grow. It is important for small businesses to truly understand this principle so they can apply it to how they present themselves to Gen Y consumers. Don't pretend to be a huge company who just has one office. Instead, be proud that you are a homegrown business.

Moreover, if you can show Gen Y that you use your profits to support other local businesses, Gen Y will be more inclined to support your business. For instance, if you can buy from a local supplier, that is great. If you go one step further and say you spend your money personally and buy local products when they are available, you are able to really show your dedication to the community. I believe this is what buying local is becoming. Sure, it is great to reduce carbon emissions, but Gen Y also embraces these practices as a way to ensure that neighbors help each other and not everyone is willing to kowtow to the conglomerates.

5. Biodegradables

I live in New York, and as a New Yorker I am constantly subjected to giant mountains of garbage. Every now and then I might find something cool sitting on the sidewalk waiting to be picked up, like a vintage coat rack. However, the vast majority of trash on the curb is just that: trash. It is mind boggling to think of how much trash this one city produces every day, and haunting to consider the amount of waste residents and visitors must produce annually. Lucky for most, twice a week, workers in jumpsuits come and remove all the trash so we can free up our minds to worry about more important things. The problem is even though the trash is no longer in our faces it doesn't disappear; quite to the contrary, much of the garbage will spend the next few hundred years occupying space in one of the many landfills.

One thing that can work to reduce all that waste is the use of biodegradable products. Many of the items that are currently being made out of plastics that will outlive us all could easily be made out of biodegradable materials. For many businesses one of the easiest ways to capitalize on this is by re-evaluating your packaging materials. There are many low-cost alternatives.

For instance, we have all received items packed in excessive amounts of packing peanuts, which are those obnoxious little Styrofoam blobs that stick to everything and get everywhere. For most people, they just go through the tedious task of gathering them all up into a pile and throwing them in the garbage and never give them another thought. The problem is that every day thousands of people ship and receive packages that are filled with those little Styrofoam bits and most people just discard them. Singularly they are rather small but collectively they take up a lot of space, (that is kind of their job in shipping), but consider that all those peanuts end up occupying space in a landfill and that they will probably be there forever. It is amazingly wasteful considering that the only reason we use them is to prevent things from banging around as we ship them. Many things can fulfill that really simple task, so why use petroleum-based, non-biodegradable pieces of Styrofoam? Instead, a business can use an inexpensive equivalent made from 100 percent natural corn or wheat starch. These packing materials are fully degradable, contain no toxins, and send a message to your customers that you are committed to going green.

Another obvious option most businesses can incorporate is to replace their plastic bags. Consider how many plastic bags you get in a year's worth of shopping. Most people throw out these bags and never think about it. Once again though, although they are forgotten, it doesn't mean they will be going anywhere anytime soon. Much like the peanuts, there

At the end of the day, going green is a growing trend.

are cornstarch alternatives that companies can use. Like biodegradable packing material, these bags will naturally decompose after being used and contribute back to the ecosystem and not poison it with harmful toxins. These are two easy options most businesses can incorporate fairly painlessly in order to go green and gain more Gen Y customers.

At the end of the day, going green is a growing trend. Every day, new companies are able to grow exponentially thanks to a dedicated eco-minded following while others lose customers due to their wasteful reputations. Gen Y is young, so we have a huge vested interest in the condition of this planet in the next 50 years. Companies need to truly understand and empathize in constructing their going green campaigns. There are almost immeasurable amounts of ways to start going green today, and many of the ways will actually save companies money as they gain new customers. Aside from that, one of the biggest reasons to go green is that this tiny rock we all occupy is all we have. I think we can all agree colonies on Mars are not going to happen anytime soon, so we better do all we can to ensure decent living conditions on this planet. Gandhi once said, "We must be the change we want to see in the world."

thirteen
HOW TO BE COOL, AND "NOT TRY TOO HARD"

The concept of "cool" is as enticing as it is intangible. It is the kind of thing that is hard to explain. Like Justice Potter Stewart once said when trying to describe "obscene" in relation to a pornography case, "I know it when I see it."

The pursuit of cool consumes many marketing campaigns. Unfortunately, much like quicksand, the harder you fight to stay cool, the deeper you sink into lame. However, it is important to note that the idea of what is cool varies between generations. This is not a particularly surprising point to many on an individual level, most would spare their kids the embarrassment of trying to act hip. To hear someone in his or her 50s reference gangster rap slang just sounds odd. Much like if your dog were to meow, the effect is both confusing and somewhat unsettling. I would know, my mother listens to much hard-core gangster rap. Hearing my mother sing along with songs that contain slang I don't even know is just weird.

However, many businesses forget this most fundamental of principles when trying to reach Gen Y consumers. They try to study what is cool in the Gen Y community and then go about trying to replicate their interpretation of cool in campaigns. However, much like when this is attempted on a personal level the results often feel forced, unoriginal, and painfully uncool.

You can't just imitate something and expect to be cool. You must take time to evaluate the root of what makes it cool.

I often see ad campaigns that were very obviously created by a room full of Baby Boomers trying to think of what the young people are into these days. What many Baby Boomers don't consider is how much do you think you would have related to an ad campaign your parents had created to target you when you were 18? No matter how much the traditionalists had studied it they wouldn't even have been able to fully replicate hippie values. You can't just imitate something and expect to be cool. You must take time to evaluate the root of what makes it cool. You must learn what they love, what they dislike, what they admire, and what they want to be. When you fully understand the values you can begin to craft a campaign that will actually resonate with Gen Y consumers.

1. Fundamental Laws of Cool

To understand what makes things cool now, we must first discover what made things cool in the past. When we look at historical trendsetters we can observe some interesting recurring traits. Such as, how was Elvis like Eminem? What was the difference between The Beatles and The Rolling Stones? How was John F. Kennedy similar to Barack Obama? Let's examine the guiding principles behind what makes things cool.

1.1 Shock and awe

A surefire way to be cool is to shock people. This is seemingly a timeless principle, the only difference is that for every generation the threshold gets higher and it takes more to shock people. Gen Y has definitely become desensitized, at least compared to previous generations. Consider one of the first motion pictures to be available with sound, *The Phantom of the Opera*; the scene where the phantom removes his mask to reveal his deformed face terrified movie audiences. The scene in question seems almost comical by modern-day standards; essentially it was a normal looking guy with bad hair and a pig nose. At the time of its release though, women were actually fainting in the theaters from the shock. Compare that to a modern-day horror film such as *28 Days Later*, a zombie film in which the zombies don't stumble about at a sluggish pace but instead viciously chase and attack their victims with all the intensity of an angry and rabid dog! If the trend of increasing expectations continues, I shudder to think what moviegoing audiences will be subjected to in 50 years.

The principle holds true that shocking people is a surefire way to become cool. To illustrate how timeless this principle is, let's compare two seemingly unrelated musical figures: Elvis and Eminem. Elvis in many respects was the foundation of modern rock music. Many people love Elvis' classic songs such as "Hound Dog" and "Heartbreak Hotel." People love these songs so much that they often forget that at the time Elvis' style was considered lewd, crass, and downright vulgar. Firstly, the music he played, rock and roll, was considered "black people music"; the term rock and roll itself is actually derived from urban slang for sexual intercourse. The idea of a white boy singing "ghetto" music was considered highly offensive to many, spurring outright protest in many religious communities. Elvis was even banned from appearing on many major TV shows. Even when he was finally allowed to be on *The Ed Sullivan Show*, he was only filmed from the waist up. The way Elvis would gyrate his hips during a song was considered especially offensive and people refused to air it.

What was the end result of all this controversy? Elvis is one of the most recognizable musical figures of all time, and people will probably still be listening to his songs 100 years from now. There were many other artists who released literally thousands of songs around the same time as Elvis, many of the songs may have been even better than what Elvis was able to create. At the end of the day though, it was the shock factor that elevated Elvis to the status of the "King of Rock and Roll."

When one considers the real factors that solidified Elvis' reputation as cool, we can see just how similar Elvis is to what I think of as Gen Y's Elvis, Eminem. The story of Marshall Mathers III, Eminem if you will, is a very interesting story that was well portrayed in the movie *8 Mile*. From humble beginnings in Detroit, Eminem was able to rise up the charts and come to define and popularize an emerging music style. Once again, a new culture had been developed in the urban lower-class communities. However, the music was no longer rock and roll, a genre that had come to be dominated by white artists in the time since Elvis. The new style was rap music. It was urban, raw, offensive, and scared the hell out of people. It had all the beginnings of the Elvis story.

Along came Eminem, who took this new emerging style that many already found offensive and he added in every last way he could think of to be vulgar and obscene. He made blatant references to intercourse; often very lewd references. He sang about killing his ex-wife. His music videos were four-minute montages of the obscene and shocking. Nothing was sacred, and he pushed the envelope further with every new album and video. What was the result of all these purposefully shocking acts? Gen Y loved him! Eminem has sold millions of records. He proved once again that shocking sells. Even in an industry as crowded and competitive as the music industry, adding shock value is a way to rise above the rest and be heard and ultimately remembered.

Ultimately, when trying to be cool it is important to remember it is all an illusion; often the truth has very little to do with the end result.

1.2 Image is everything

Image is important; in fact, it is everything when trying to define cool. Albert Einstein once said, "Reality is merely an illusion, albeit a very persistent one." How we perceive things often has very little to do with the truth. A great example of this would be the difference between The Beatles and The Rolling Stones. The Beatles were considered teenybopper material. They graced the cover of magazines like *Tiger Beat*, and young girls would swoon over the pictures. They were the Jonas Brothers of their day, which is a little too much of a compliment to the Jonas Brothers. The Rolling Stones, by comparison, were the bad boys. They were the originators of the sex, drugs, and rock and roll philosophy.

On the one hand, The Beatles were born and raised in Liverpool, which was a pretty rough port town in the north of England. Since The Beatles, the town has enjoyed the benefits of an artistic resurgence as a direct result of The Beatles being from there. However, when The Beatles were growing up there it was still a pretty tough town, not unlike growing up in present-day Detroit.

The Rolling Stones, on the other hand, were all from upper-middle class families with a few of them being born in Dartford, England. They didn't have to grow up tough, they had pretty stable backgrounds, but they acted tough. In the Gen Y community this would be considered being a "poser," pretending to be something you are not.

But never mind the actual history behind these two legendary bands, the image of each band persists to this day. When you think of The Beatles, you remember four men in matching suits singing on *The Ed Sullivan Show* to screaming young girls. The Rolling Stones are remembered as the bad boys who wrecked hotel rooms with wild and crazy parties. Ultimately, when trying to be cool it is important to remember it is all an illusion; often the truth has very little to do with the end result.

1.3 Charisma

An undying principle in cool is charisma. Many of the defining characters of history have had charisma, that certain quality that just drew other people to them like moths to a flame. In fact, one of the first producers to ever give Tom Hanks, then an unknown actor, a chance, did so because he said he had a certain quality and people couldn't help but like him.

Bill Maher defined my personal favorite explanation of the charisma quality when he was talking about Charlie Sheen. He said, "[Charlie Sheen] could beat a nun to death on a pile of dead puppies, and

America would just go, 'Oh, that Charlie! We love him.'" Considering all the scandals Charlie Sheen has been involved in, Maher might have a point. After all, this is the same guy who paid for his prostitutes with a check to Heidi Fleiss, yet he is still on the prime time sitcom *Two and a Half Men*. The former politician, Eliot Spitzer, wasn't so lucky and may not have much charisma considering his clandestine affairs married his career faster than you can say Monica Lewinsky! Even Bill Clinton was able to use his immutable charisma to dodge impeachment after the Kenneth Starr report.

For the best example of the outmost of charisma in the oval office we must look back to the 1960s. John F. Kennedy (JFK) was in many respects the essence of charisma, he was the youngest elected president at the time, and moreover he was the first Catholic to be president. This seems like a minuscule fact now, but in those days it was a really big deal. How was one man able to break so many boundaries in the most established institution in the nation? In a word, charisma. When JFK spoke, people couldn't help but listen. Many of the speeches he gave during his short time in office still resonate with people. He is quoted and paraphrased by politicians almost as much as the bible. His charisma was so strong he was able to unify the nation and bring people together to accomplish amazing things.

Another recent figurehead to emerge has been President Barack Obama. Much in the same way as JFK, Obama was able to shatter boundaries by being the first African American to be elected President. Moreover, much like JFK, President Obama was able to bring the country to a feverish pitch during the elections. When President Obama speaks people really listen and believe what he is saying. He has a way of invigorating people and speaking to them on a level that is both personal and logical. I know personally when I hear him speak I often find myself nodding in agreement.

Like JFK, President Obama is able to use his inherent charisma to convey a message that truly resonates with the masses. For companies, this is an important lesson in cool. Ultimately, having an individual who can act as a spokesperson with charisma can advance a company in the category of cool, much faster than most other methods. A figure like President Obama has a certain power, where when he speaks people want to listen. Now I know many will think, "Yeah, but those are politicians, and the dynamics of politics and business marketing are much different." To which, I would say two things. First, don't be so negative, you pessimist; and second, Steve Jobs.

Steve Jobs articulates quite well how a company can rise and fall based on the charisma of just one person. Jobs is the chief executive officer (CEO) and founder of Apple Inc. computers, which if you have been paying any attention to this book thus far you might be starting to appreciate the depth of my love of all things Apple. One big reason for this, I must confess, is the sheer genius and charisma of Jobs.

Many of you may be quite familiar with Jobs' almost cliché presentations of new Apple products. Donning a black turtleneck and with a killer slide show presentation, Jobs personally presents each and every new Apple product. At the end of one of these presentations I can't help but to feel that I absolutely *need* whatever he is selling. I often consider the following types of questions: How did I ever live without a phone that could listen to a song and tell me the name of the song and who wrote it? How can I live without a laptop so slim it will fit into an envelope?

Now I know the pessimists among us might still speculate, "Well, Apple does well because they are just a great company, it isn't just because of the character of Steve Jobs." However, Apple presents a unique exemplification of this point because there was in fact a period of time when Apple was sans-Jobs. In 1985, the other board members had a power struggle with Jobs and in the end he resigned from his own company. During the period without Jobs, the company was brought to its knees. In fact, the company was only saved from bankruptcy by a huge investment from Bill Gates' company, Microsoft.

In 1997, Jobs returned and bought out Apple Computer Inc. In the more than ten years since Jobs' return, Apple has gone from needing a Microsoft bailout to stay in business to being the number-one computer company. In fact, the main question today in computers is, "Do you use a Mac or PC?" People forget though that PC encompasses literally dozens of other companies, whereas Mac is just one single company. Moreover, as I look around the Starbucks where I am currently writing, over half the people here are on Mac computers, including me.

2. What Is Cool to Gen Y?

Now that we have established some of the timeless qualities that define cool, lets examine some aspects that Gen Y specifically finds cool. What traits do they genuinely extol and want to identify themselves with? What do they seek to replicate in themselves and present as part of themselves to be perceived as cool to other members of Gen Y? Why is Gen Y obsessed with quoting *Family Guy*? Why does Gen Y pay good money to see a documentary by a former vice president, who historically has been about as entertaining as an algebra textbook?

2.1 Giggity Giggity

If you are a member of Gen Y, you probably recognize the words "Giggity Giggity" as a *Family Guy* quote, the catch phrase of the character Quagmire. Many members of Gen Y love *Family Guy*. We quote it incessantly, and our humor in general mirrors the humor of the show. Even those who don't avidly watch the show are aware of it and have probably been forced to watch a few episodes. People like me go to great lengths to watch *Family Guy*, and proudly quote and reference the show whenever possible. The reason is *Family Guy* is cool. The show embodies something Gen Y loves: humor. In my opinion, the show is well written and the jokes are very witty, not just slapstick.

Clever humor is a great way to be seen as cool by Gen Y.

Clever humor is a great way to be seen as cool by Gen Y. If you can mimic the style of *Family Guy* in your advertisements Gen Y will readily identify with them. Obviously if we use quotes from *Family Guy* and mimic the show's humor as a way to identify ourselves as cool, the same principle can be applied for companies trying to reach Gen Y. This is also advantageous to companies for the simple reason it is hard to reach Gen Y through traditional media sources, but if you use the *Family Guy* style comedy, Gen Y will go online and seek you out.

Burger King and Priceline went so far as to sponsor Seth MacFarlane, the creator of *Family Guy*, to make a few cartoon clips to air on YouTube. Before the clip, there would be a short five-second cartoon endorsing Burger King or Priceline. The Burger King ad showed "The King" being pursued by the apes from *Planet of the Apes*. Did it make sense? Nope, but irreverence has always been one of the keys to the *Family Guy* show's success. The Priceline ad showed a cartoon William Shatner in a hotel calling down to the lobby calmly threatening the staff he'll use "the nunchakus" if he didn't get more towels. Once again classic *Family Guy*-style comedy, even in the ads before the actual sketch. The sketches were drawn in the same style as *Family Guy*, but didn't feature any of the show's characters. Of course, I watched all the clips online and then forwarded the links to my friends so they could watch the clips as well.

This is actually a great example of viral marketing, because Gen Y spreads the content throughout the community themselves. Why wouldn't they? They love *Family Guy*, and the clips on the Internet are often a little edgier than what Fox allows to be shown on the TV show.

Though it doesn't necessarily have to be exactly *Family Guy* to catch Gen Y's attention, as was shown for the Gillette ad campaign, "Fight for Kisses." The ad prefaces by saying that for years babies have been stealing all the kisses from their mothers because of their super soft skin, leaving the poor fathers to feel neglected. But now dads everywhere have a new secret weapon: Gillette razors. The shave leaves men's skin so smooth that now they get all the kisses. This leaves the baby in the ad bitter and it showed him training like a boxer, preparing for the fight for kisses. The ad was animated; obviously a real baby couldn't jump rope or hit a punching bag, which made it feel a little like *Family Guy*. Also the ad featured a determined baby doing un-babylike things, much like what is found on *Family Guy*. The whole ad was irreverent and funny just the kind of thing Gen Y loves. As a result the ad was a huge hit with Gen Y. I had a few friends send me links to watch the commercial online.

2.2 Boring presidential candidate to movie star

In 2000, Al Gore led a presidential campaign that was about as cool as picking up your date in your mom's minivan. I supported him because I am a hopeless Democrat by nature, but if not for party allegiance I would have been hard pressed to find another reason to support him. After all, this is the same guy whose wife, in the 1980s, led the charge to censor music in America. There was a huge deposition, a witch-hunt almost, where all the popular musicians of the '80s came to try to defend their right to freedom of speech. Even John Denver spoke out against what Tipper Gore was trying to do. When even John Denver thinks you are being too uptight that really says something! The man who sang about sunshine on his shoulders making him happy thought Tipper Gore was being too much of a square!

Even *The Simpsons* in the late '90s got in a shot about what a bore Al Gore was. In one episode Lisa buys a copy of Al Gore's book *Sane Planning, Sensible Tomorrow* (not a real book) and when word gets back to The White House, an intern runs into Al Gore's office and exclaims, "Mr. Vice President! Great news, someone finally bought a copy of your book!" To which Al Gore replies in monotone, "Well that is good news, this calls for a celebration." He puts on a record of the song "Celebration" by Kool and the Gang. As the chorus sings "Celebrate good times," he unenthusiastically says, "I will."

In many ways the jokes made on *The Simpsons* have been a social barometer as to how Gen Y feels about any given pop-culture figure. It goes without saying that in the late '90s Al Gore wasn't riding too high on most Gen Ys' lists of celebrities they would like to spend an evening with. How then was Al Gore able to drastically turn around his lackluster public image to being one of the most followed figures on Twitter?

He conveniently used *An Inconvenient Truth*, which is a movie about the effects of global warming, and I think I can say without hyperbole that it remains one of the greatest sources for information on global warming. Unlike Al Gore, the film was both interesting and highly entertaining. The film had many aspects that made it highly attractive to Gen Y. It felt very genuine and real with most of the footage being of Al Gore giving a presentation at a college campus.

The overall production value was not overly high, which gave the documentary a very organic feel. It allowed viewers to feel they were being made to focus on the issue at hand and not the production value. Also, the movie focused entirely on an issue that is very important to almost all members of Gen Y: global warming. The movie even featured a small clip from *The Simpsons* to illustrate the greenhouse effect. By way of communicating to Gen Y, the movie was extremely effective. As a result, Gen Y spread word of the film by word of mouth like wildfire. The movie remains one of the top-grossing documentaries of all time, and its corresponding book was a best-seller, which is a huge improvement over his fictitious book that was only bought by Lisa Simpson!

Al Gore was able to seemingly do the impossible; he completely turned his image around in the minds of Gen Y within a few short years. He did so by applying one of Gen Y's elements of being cool by being a passionate advocate for a cause they care about. Gen Y, like most, admire a selfless dedication in someone, especially if it is in relation to a cause they support.

Fortunately for businesses this principle can transcend from an individual to be applied to the perception of an entire company. An organization can be dedicated to a cause just as easily as an individual can be. For example, the organization People for the Ethical Treatment of Animals (PETA), has achieved a celebrity status and most people would be hard pressed to name the founder of the organization. The important thing to remember is to take a cause passionately and take steps to raise awareness to help make it better. If you can do this well, you can be as cool to Gen Y as the new and improved Al Gore (or something even better).

The important thing to remember is to take a cause passionately and take steps to raise awareness to help make it better.

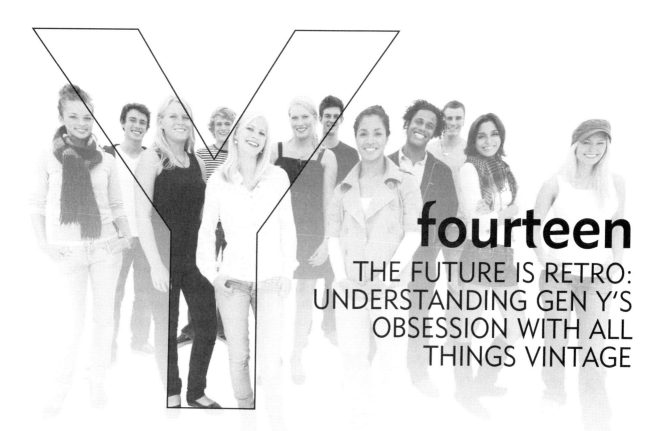

fourteen
THE FUTURE IS RETRO: UNDERSTANDING GEN Y'S OBSESSION WITH ALL THINGS VINTAGE

Recently I was walking through a clothing store in London called Top Male. The store is not unlike other modern clothing stores in Europe in that it seemed overpriced to me and the styles tested the boundaries of my masculinity. However, on this trip I did find one thing that surprised me. Many of the season's new looks were popular clothing fads from the late 1980s and early 1990s. All the usual suspects were there: brightly colored neon clothing, cheap neon hats, and parachute pants so ugly they would have made MC Hammer cringe. They even had Reebok shoes with the built-in pump that I wanted so badly growing up but my mom wouldn't buy for me because she claimed, "You will just grow out of them in a month." Considering my final shoe size ended up being 13, she may have had a point after all!

It is an odd feeling seeing the trends you grew up with being presented as retro fashion. It's the kind of thing that makes a person feel really old and ponder just what he or she has done with his or her life. My existential funk aside, it is unusual to see fashions that are only 15 years old being reintroduced already. Usually it takes at least one generation before something can be considered cool again. Like finding your dad's jacket in the attic that he used to wear when he was your age. By comparison I certainly wasn't old enough to be the father of any of the shoppers at Top Male, as I was barely old enough to be their older brother.

Gen Y loves all things vintage and retailers are always quick to pick up on these trends and cater to them.

Why the quick turnaround on trends these days? Why are we seeing a resurgence of 1990s culture when there is only just over a decade between then and now? The reason is because Gen Y loves all things vintage and retailers are always quick to pick up on these trends and cater to them. With only so many fashion items to pick from in the '60s through the '80s the next logical step for clothing companies was to crack the seal on the '90s. If you want to reach Gen Y consumers, take a page from the clothing companies' game plan and look forward by looking backward.

1. Reasons Gen Y Loves Retro Items

Time and time again Gen Y goes out of their way to buy items that are vintage. Even advertisements that have a vintage feel are exponentially more appealing and thus more able to cut through the noise when trying to reach Gen Y, but where did this fascination with nostalgia come from?

1.1 Gen Ys are close with their parents

Gen Y more so than any generation before it has an extremely close relationship with parents and always has. Our parents were more than just the ones who paid for our food and shelter; they were also our good friends. Like most people who are friends with someone much older than them, we inevitably emulated a lot of their traits. Our parents were more likely to sit down with us and show us old photos of their friends and them. Because of this closeness we have developed more of an obsession for all the old nostalgic items that are from before our time.

I remember being quite young and seeing pictures of one of my uncles and his 1960s muscle car. I remember thinking, wow, my lame uncle used to be cool? I thought to myself, I wish I owned a muscle car just like that so I could be cool. As a result my first car was a 1978 Camaro. I had the car painted black with two white racing stripes, which led to its nickname among my friends, "the Skunk." Of course, the odor of the interior probably contributed a bit to that nickname too! I loved my classic muscle car and it did make me feel very cool, when it was actually running that is. The Skunk also taught me the first rule of owning a classic car, which is an old car creates new problems.

I have since owned all kinds of classic cars and motorcycles, and it definitely wasn't for their reliability. The reason has a lot to do with being inundated with the tastes and styles of my parents from an early age. This is the case with most of Gen Y. This presents a convenient opportunity for Baby Boomers trying to reach Gen Y consumers. You can just think back to what was cool for you when you were 18 and odds are it might still be cool to Gen Y.

What former generations found cool can actually apply to more things than just muscle cars. As stated before, clothing is one example, but also the very advertisements themselves can be retro. One company that had great success with a classic ad campaign was Volkswagen (VW). To celebrate the company's 60-year anniversary, VW released a series of ads similar to the ads they released in the '60s, but targeted at Gen Y consumers. The ads featured a picture of the original VW bus that was so popular with Baby Boomers during their hippie phase and had a slogan similar to: "It's unusual to drive the vehicle you were conceived in." The ads were very effective in reaching Gen Y consumers and personally made me want to find one of the vans. I think they should have released a replica of the classic van to go alongside the popular campaign.

1.2 Retro is unique

Gen Y has grown up in a world swamped with options. With all our options it is actually really hard to find something genuinely unique except in vintage items. Thanks to modern mass-production tactics the odds that any new item will be a one-of-a-kind are pretty slim. There have been many times I have seen another guy wearing the exact same shirt as me, which is always awkward and makes me go out of my way to not stand near my fashion twin. However, with vintage clothing items, the odds someone will have the same 1962 leather jacket are much slimmer, and within the Gen Y community we place a huge premium on individuality. The same goes for classic cars. I have owned some pretty nice new cars like a Corvette, Range Rover, and Navigator; but I have never gotten more compliments and head turns than when I was driving one of my classic cars. Even the Skunk was complimented a couple times a week and I initially bought that car for only $500.

No matter how much you spend on a new item it will never have the character of an item from yesteryear. Although one company that capitalizes on Gen Y's obsession with vintage in order to sell new items is Fender, which sells guitars. Fender saw that many people were overlooking its brand new guitars and instead seeking out and paying almost three times as much for its guitars from the '60s. In response, Fender released the relic series. The guitars were built to the exact specifications of the 1960s models, and to go that extra mile it even factory-aged the instruments so that they would be worn down in the areas that a guitar that was 40 years old would be. The guitar looked just like a vintage guitar, sounded like a vintage, but was half the price of a vintage guitar. The price was still 50 percent higher than Fender's usual price, which was music to the company's ears.

Another reason Gen Y loves vintage is because it just feels classier.

Many companies have used similar tactics to sell products to Gen Y. In fact in the denim world the practice has almost become more popular than selling jeans that aren't worn down in any way. Sometimes I see a pair of jeans that are in such rough shape I think to myself if I owned them I would throw them out, and yet they are brand new on a rack at Hollister.

1.3 Vintage feels classier

Another reason Gen Y loves vintage is because it just feels classier. We feel wearing a jacket that is from the 1960s makes a statement about us. I can't help to feel that someone who owns a lot of vintage clothing is more sophisticated. I even own a record player and a massive LP collection. I love sitting around listening to my old records. I proudly do so when I have my friends over. I could just as easily pull out my iPod and connect it to my speaker stand, which is usually how I listen to music when I am alone. But when I have company over I like bringing out the records because I think it shows depth on my part. I am not alone in this view either, most of my Gen Y friends love my record player, and I notice that they too feel more chic when we are listening to it. It is not that it is better technology; having to get up to flip the record reminds me of why music companies moved away from this technology in the first place. Also, the records tend to squeak every now and then and I am constantly forgetting to turn off the player when I go to bed, leaving the needle running all night.

The same is true for cars. There is just something about seeing someone in a car from the '50s that screams "good taste." The individual could not know the first thing about the car and maybe just bought it because he or she likes the color, but Gen Y will applaud the person's good taste. Moreover, classic cars exemplify another asset in reaching Gen Y consumers: Vintage gets looks. I have driven many cars, but no car no matter how expensive can get as many looks as a classic car. Surprisingly though, it is not even the older generations that are the most fascinated with these classic machines, it is people 16 to 29 who are the most mesmerized by these cars. People will literally turn all the way around in their seats to look at these cars, and point them out to friends.

This is a good metaphor for the value of nostalgia in general in reaching Gen Y consumers. On the one hand, companies can go out and spend $90,000 on a new Corvette and will get a few looks from those who appreciate that kind of vehicle. On the other hand, companies can spend $25,000 on a replica of a 1964 Shelby Cobra Roadster. Both cars are new, but the replica car looks and feels like a vintage item, so as a result it will turn heads all day long and get the attention of every Gen Y member it passes. Whereas the Corvette, that costs almost four times as much, can drive by relatively unnoticed because it blends into the background. The 1964 Cobra can cut through all the noise better than its more expensive counterpart could ever hope to.

This is not unlike marketing campaigns. All the companies are busy trying to spend the most money to create the finest campaign. Like the Corvette, the campaign might be great on paper, well designed using all the newest technologies, but at the end of the day when all your competitors are also designing their campaigns the same way, you will end up being just another fast Corvette on the road that nobody notices. Adding a retro element, like the replica Roadster, gives you an edge and enables your company to stand out. Even when the item is not in fact vintage but just looks and feels vintage it can be enough to stand out for substantially less money.

1.4 Owning vintage makes Gen Y feel smarter

One of the main reasons Gen Y has been so quick to adapt retro trends is it is a way to feel more intelligent. I refer back to my squeaky record player, I will listen to it with my Gen Y friends and we will all remark on how much warmer the sound is. However, the ugly skeleton in my closet is that I can't tell the difference, but I am plenty happy to sit back and revel in people assuming I am more intelligent than I really am.

Gen Y prides ourselves on being savvy. What better way to appear savvy than to enjoy items most don't use and then justify the use of outdated technology by making vague references to the "feel" or "soul" of the items. "They just don't make them like this anymore," we will say, patting ourselves on the back. Of course they don't; manufacturing technology has had almost half a century to advance so that they don't have to make them like that anymore. As is the case with my record player and the Skunk, the modern replacements are much better made. However, we still take pleasure in claiming that our use of vintage is indicative of our higher intelligence.

Moreover, the act of finding these vintage items plays on yet another one of Gen Y's fascinations, the love of being a savvy shopper. We love doing research on new products to find the best one, and adding vintage to that pursuit increases the challenge and bragging rights exponentially. When I find a good item at a thrift store, I am much happier with the item than if I had bought it new. I even feel compelled to tell everyone that I got it from a secondhand shop, which is odd because thrift stores were initially started for low-income people to buy items secondhand.

For most businesses the vintage appeal can be incorporated into marketing and some packaging.

As a result, most people wouldn't brag about having to shop at one. By comparison, Gen Y is almost unable to stop talking about shopping at secondhand stores.

1.5 Vintage = recycled

A final reason Gen Y loves vintage so much is that it is a way of recycling. Instead of constantly making new clothes and casting aside "outdated" clothing every two years, only to tax our resources to produce new fashions, is wasteful. Why not buy the clothes that have already been made? There really is something to be said about the phrase "one person's trash is another person's treasure." Instead of just throwing out items to rot in a garbage dump, why not give them a shot at a second life as a vintage item? Since most of Gen Y is highly eco-minded this plays a large role in their love of buying vintage items, after all for every T-shirt that is bought secondhand that means one less T-shirt needs to be made.

2. How Can Companies Use These Principles to Reach Gen Y?

Companies can use these principles in a variety of ways when trying to reach Gen Y. The obvious option is following Fender's example and producing products with a vintage appeal. Items can be factory worn to give them the feel of being aged. Also it is important to use the materials of a vintage item. However, this is obviously not practical for many businesses. For most businesses the vintage appeal can be incorporated into marketing and some packaging.

2.1 Packaging

Packaging is an easy option to change for many businesses. Moreover, many businesses forget what a huge impact packaging has on the customer experience. Steve Jobs spends a large amount of time ensuring that the packaging of an Apple product is a big part of the positive customer experience.

Businesses can create packaging that has a retro look, such as when General Mills released many of its popular cereals in boxes with their original designs. This was a great move, because not only are the old box designs vintage, the lack of clutter the old designs featured really helped them stand out on crowded cereal shelves. This is also a fairly easy endeavor because instead of coming up with a new idea altogether you can just borrow ideas from vintage packaging.

2.2 Marketing

Probably the simplest and most effective way to incorporate nostalgia into any existing business model is to add it to the marketing plan. Most businesses are constantly transitioning to new ad campaigns, or at least they should be, so it is simple enough to just give one of those campaigns the look of vintage posters.

M&M's had great success with using something that looked vintage when they introduced a campaign that featured the cartoon spokesperson "Red," in what looked like a vintage World War II Soviet propaganda poster. I have actually seen the ad being sold on T-shirts at major retailers, so obviously the company was able to effectively tap into Gen Y's love of retro with the ad.

At the end of the day, one of the greatest advantages this retro fad affords companies is the opportunity to be different without having to be very creative. Companies can use vintage ads and products as a template and develop a "new" look. Moreover, there is a degree of certainty in designing a retro campaign. When a company tries to introduce something as the "most modern and hip" item there is a chance it just won't catch on. However, leveraging Gen Y's love of all things vintage enables companies to create ads and products that have a much higher chance of catching on, because the vintage element has already been established as cool in the minds of Gen Y. It is like the old proverb says, "The more things change, the more they stay the same."

Y

fifteen
APPEALING TO GEN Y'S INTELLECTUAL SIDE

The old cliché of the "friendless bookworm" has ceased to exist in Gen Y's life. Very often in our school days the kids with the highest marks were also the most popular. By stark contrast to previous stereotypes most members of Gen Y feel compelled to be intellectually astute. More and more members of Gen Y struggle to prove their cognitive aptitude. It is no longer just about being good at sports or being pretty, Gen Y members feel the need to be rounded out with brains too. It is odd to see people who are obviously less-than-gifted thinkers trying very hard to pass themselves off as philosophic souls. Not unlike watching a dog shake hands, it is cute to watch but I still wouldn't believe him or her as a businessperson.

Indeed the paradigm has shifted with Gen Y. In former generations, kids who spent all their time at libraries were considered social outcasts. They were perceived to be bad at sports, and socially awkward. The stigma is prevalent throughout many movies from previous generations. We have all seen the Hollywood stereotype: a "nerdy" character donning thick-framed glasses and a cardigan. Ironically, with Gen Y these items have actually become trendy. There has even been a fashion movement called "geek chic." Nerdy isn't nerdy anymore, in fact it has become the height of coolness.

1. Why Brains Surpassed Brawn

Gen Y valuing brains over all other traits is a result of a multitude of changes that occurred during their formative years. It is true that students have always been graded and thus there is a natural pressure to get good grades and work to achieve higher marks than those around them. As human beings we are inherently competitive so this has existed to a veritable extent throughout all generations. With Gen Y the pressure to be smart was much higher, it wasn't seen merely as a favorable attribute so much as the bane of every Gen Y's existence.

Gen Ys grew up believing that dropping out of school was akin to social suicide, that one might as well just jump off a bridge before he or she drops out of high school. Moreover, if the person didn't achieve higher than average grades, there must have been a problem with him or her. Gen Y ceased to have dumb kids; instead, anyone who performed poorly on tests was suffering from attention-deficit hyperactivity disorder (ADHD), and had to be medicated accordingly. Consider for a moment that Gen Ys grew up in a world where if the person wasn't getting above-average grades it meant he or she was broken and that there was something terribly wrong with him or her. Of course, this is ignoring the fact that in order to have a statistical curve on which to judge who is above average there needs to be an average and a below average. If Gen Ys were to all be "above average" that would be the new average and no one would be above average. Gen Ys grew up in a world where everyone had to be smart at every subject, no exceptions.

What was the source of this almost irrational obsession with intelligence?

1.1 Parents

Gen Y was blessed to have some of the most attentive parents of any generation. However, an unfortunate side effect of parents of Gen Ys is heightened expectations. Parents would examine and scrutinize each and every report card. When marks dropped the parents quickly sought to remedy the problem. In fact, in my high school whenever a student was getting lower than a C in any course halfway through the year, the parents of the student had to come in and meet with the guidance counselor to figure out what needed to be done about this atrocity of a below-average grade. Consider the message this sent to Gen Y's psychology. If you aren't smart, someone will tell your parents you are an idiot and make them come in and meet with your counselor to figure out how to fix you. The ramifications of this resulted in Gen Y placing a large amount of emphasis on the importance of being smart.

Even after graduation and moving out of our parents' house we continued to have the mind-set of "I am intelligent and I need to be able to show it."

1.2 Tougher economic times

Our parents were not misguided in pushing us to achieve more in school, ultimately times have gotten tougher. My grandfather could have dropped out of high school, gotten a job at a factory, and still been able to provide a decent living for himself and his family. This is obviously no longer the case. Even having a high school diploma doesn't mean much these days. Telling a potential employer you have a high school diploma is about as impressive as telling him or her you have the ability to turn oxygen into carbon dioxide.

Going to college no longer seems like an elective activity. I remember asking some of my friends why they were going to college, and they would often say, "I don't know, it is just what you are supposed to do after high school." Inspiring, isn't it? High school students seek higher education much like one regards brushing his or her teeth at night, a matter of routine and obligation. However, it is important to note this sense of obligation is typical of Gen Y's view on intelligence in general.

2. How You Can Use Gen Y's Need to Be Smart

In a way, the Gen Y need to feel smart is their Achilles' heel. By catering to their strong sense of intellect companies can predictably influence Gen Y's purchasing habits.

2.1 Reinforcing Gen Y's intellect

Gen Y craves constant reinforcement of our intellect. In school we were constantly rated and graded, so now even the oldest of Gen Y who is no longer in school still craves that level of reinforcement of intellectual prowess. This affords great opportunities to companies trying to reach Gen Y consumers. Any campaign that strokes Gen Y's ego and allows us to feel intelligent will do exponentially better than a campaign that doesn't.

I recently saw an ad for a printer company that was offering a $50 rebate when the customer traded in his or her old inefficient printer for a brand new efficient printer. The ad admonished the would-be consumer to make the "intelligent choice." The exact wording was genius because it granted the consumer the intellectual high ground. The implied message was that by doing what the company wants you to do, you are

By catering to their strong sense of intellect companies can predictably influence Gen Y's purchasing habits.

showing what an intelligent consumer you are. Something as simple as a slight change in wording can have huge impact on ad effectiveness.

Gen Y wants to feel that they are making the most savvy, smartest decision. I believe many companies fail to properly acknowledge this when trying to reach Gen Y. Many campaigns' copywriting still feels preachy and explanatory. The businesses feel they need to explain the product fully and quite simply in order to be able to attract consumers. However, with Gen Y, companies may be having the exact opposite of the intended effect.

Many companies tend to write their sales materials for the dumbest person to understand. Everything is over-explained, and worded so simply that even a toddler could perceive the material as condescending. Businesses are afraid that if the consumers don't fully understand the message, they won't be inclined to purchase the products.

2.2 Not catering to the bottom 10 percent

The problem is when companies write their materials to be understood by the bottom 10 percent of the intelligence curve, they risk offending the other 90 percent. Moreover, with Gen Y we demand to feel smart, and an ad campaign that feels it necessary to walk us through every baby step of the product doesn't make us feel like the geniuses we view ourselves as, but rather like blithering idiots. As you remember, Gen Y feels so compelled to be smart, we were taught that being below average in intelligence means we are "broken or need to be fixed." When you consider a very basic explanation in advertising you can see that the derived message to Gen Y is that we are "broken," which is highly offensive and definitely not a good way to gain us as customers.

In a way, we are highly sensitive about our intelligence. Talking to Gen Y in a very basic manner is extremely insulting, even when the business is trying to be helpful. Most weight-loss clinics wouldn't advertise to potential customers, "Tired of Being Tubby?" The phrase is not outwardly offensive, but when a group is already sensitive about a topic it is best to tread lightly. Many companies that deal with weight loss beat around the bush so much it becomes hard to even know what they are selling. Yet when it comes to Gen Y's sensitivity about their IQ, companies persistently and consistently release materials that are metaphorically asking us if we have put on a few pounds, then they are perplexed as to why they don't gain new Gen Y customers.

2.3 Mind your wording

Companies should speak to Gen Y consumers with the assumption that the consumers have intelligence and not ineptitude — the bottom 10 percent be damned! Let's face it, the bottom 10 percent are used to not fully understanding things, so do not annoy the other 90 percent by spoon-feeding them information. Instead, companies should do the exact opposite of the current protocol.

You should talk to Gen Y consumers just as you would talk to another person of the utmost capabilities and mental faculties.

You should talk to Gen Y consumers just as you would talk to another person of the utmost capabilities and mental faculties. Salespeople have been using this trick for years, to great success. Instead of lecturing clients on the benefits of a product, a good salesperson will reference the customer in a way that assumes the listener already understands what he or she is saying. Let's compare two examples, the first is a lecturing pitch, the second assumes the listener is intelligent and knowledgeable.

"You probably didn't know but this car comes with a five-year warranty. The warranty covers the engine and powertrain. You should know that it is the best warranty of all the other manufactures. You should definitely really think about how important a good warranty is when buying a new car."

This is not an overly offensive thing for a car salesperson to say. In this example, he is trying to be helpful and express the benefits of the warranty to the customer. However, he explains the benefits like the customer doesn't have a clue about warranties or that they are important to think about when purchasing a car. Now compare the second pitch to the previous pitch, but this time we will give the customer the intellectual high ground.

"I am sure you know all about our industry leading five-year warranty that covers the engine and powertrain. It's funny how other people who come here have no idea how important a good warranty is when buying a new car."

The customer gets the same message either way, but the second time the salesperson is able to inform the customer and pay his or her intelligence a compliment at the same time. The statement assumes intelligence on the listener's part, and even if the customer doesn't know about the warranty and how important it is, now he or she does, all without having to feel like he or she was talked down to or just lectured. The difference may seem slight but when it comes to appealing to Gen Y consumers it is huge. If you can pay a compliment to Gen Y's intellect, or make them feel that in buying your product they are making a logical decision, you will have much a higher rate of return with Gen Y customers.

Businesses trying to reach Gen Y must be mindful of this principle in all communications with Gen Y. Little differences can have huge ramifications because no detail is too small to consider. Even as I am writing this I am listening to music on Pandora Internet radio, an online music provider. How Pandora works is you put in the name of an artist or song that you like and it will play a list of songs that are similar to that one in nature. It is usually uncanny in its assumptions of what other songs I would like, but every now and then it plays one I don't like. I have the option to hit the next button or hit the "I Don't Like This" button that will tell the program to not play music like that song in the future. The system is genius; however, even more impressive is the message displayed when an error message occurs. Instead of just an error message it says, "A problem occurred when carrying out your request. It is my fault."

The difference in those four little words is huge. Pandora obviously realizes that its key demographic is Gen Y consumers. Instead of just displaying its error message, it goes that extra little bit to assure Gen Y listeners that it wasn't the consumer's mistake, it was the company's fault. An obvious by-product of our need to be "above average" is a slight perfectionist tendency. Those four little words account for Gen Y's perfectionism and immediately point the blame at itself, leaving Gen Y to feel superior; not unlike an employee who quickly admits fault and enables the boss to feel gracious for forgiving the person's minor shortcoming.

At the end of the day, the issue of Gen Y's need to feel intellectually superior is an issue of minor semantics, which has very large ramifications on influencing purchasing habits. This is a tendency that has been hardwired into us from a very early age and now it is this huge festering insecurity that requires constant reinforcement. Companies that take the time to carefully word their communications will enjoy the benefits of many new customers, whereas companies that accidentally flare up this insecurity risk losing customers who may have been intrigued enough by the company to seek out its website, only to be put off by condescending materials. The smartest thing any company can do is to make Gen Y feel smart.

sixteen
SEX STILL SELLS

Despite all of our advances evolutionarily speaking, we are all still just apes in nice clothing. Thus, the most primitive of motivators still easily sways us. The concept of using attractive individuals to pitch products is not going anywhere anytime soon, for one simple reason: It works.

With Gen Y an interesting new trend has begun to emerge in this oldest of persuasion techniques. Now the products and the companies themselves have started to adopt sex appeal. The next logical step in the evolution of sexy advertising is, instead of the products being sexy by association simply because they are strategically placed next to an attractive person, now the products can have their own sex appeal. After all, sex appeal is an esoteric item that even in people often has to do with more than just physical appearance. Most would agree that Hugh Hefner is probably not the most physically attractive person in the world, and yet he is still able to measure his current girlfriends in multiples of three. Okay, perhaps he was too easy a target, seeing as his job is to be surrounded by attractive women.

What about rock stars? Some former garage band geeks tend to do very well with the ladies. Many are as awkward in appearances as they are in mannerisms, yet they have supermodels fighting over them. Nerdy college professors have students develop crushes on them. How come people in relationships seem more appealing than those who are single and available?

Obviously attraction is a complicated emotion. There is no difference when it comes to what attracts people to products or companies. Therefore, companies trying to stand out in a crowded marketplace can use these same principles to attract Gen Y consumers. First you must evaluate the root of these levels of attraction to be able to fully understand how you can apply them to your company and product.

1. The Playboy Factor

What is the mysterious force that draws so many women to Hugh Hefner? It obviously isn't his looks anymore; the idea of him naked is frankly haunting. Moreover, even if you look at pictures of him when he was younger, he was never that appealing. He kind of reminds me of an overly self-assured, grown-up alpha male. Why the appeal, and why to such an extreme? Many would argue it is his money, but this is shortsighted. There is no shortage of rich old men that are likely to manipulate young women into playing down the clock with them in order to rob their bratty kids of an inheritance! With Hugh Hefner another principle is at play which companies can use to increase their appeal. Hugh Hefner was able to become sexy by association. He was always seen with the most beautiful women in the world and eventually people just associated him with that sex appeal by default.

The root of the "sex sells" advertising is that companies have attractive people in their ads to become sexy by association. However, in attempts to reach Gen Y consumers, this old model is too one-dimensional, and it isn't good enough to just have a picture of a sexy model in a print ad. Much like Hugh Hefner, a company must learn how to inundate its image with sexy, so much so that people viewing that company can't help but make the association. Although that doesn't mean you should fire your current staff and hire nothing but models, because remember sexy is more than skin deep. To be able to fully inundate Gen Y consumers with sexy, you must discover the other alienable rules of sex appeal.

2. Party Like a Rock Star

Rock stars seem to be the very essence of a paradox. They seem to me to be generally really nerdy guys, who take up an instrument solely because they have so much free time on their hands from their total lack of social life. When they get good and write amazing songs people will gladly pay hundreds of dollars to sit in the same auditorium as a person they probably wouldn't have wanted to share a bus seat with five years earlier. Even once they have achieved fame, most rock stars are pretty odd-looking people, with exaggerated features and skinny frail frames, which serve to remind us why these guys went into music and not modeling or sports. However, these unattractive traits magically stop mattering when they are on stage singing our favorite songs.

What changes between being an awkward teenager who can't get any dates to being an awkward adult like John Mayer who can't decide between Jennifer Aniston and Jessica Simpson? The difference is the sex appeal of talent. Evolutionary scientists have suggested that we actually developed artistic talents as a means of attracting mates. It only makes sense that displaying talent would play a role in attraction. This principle is not reserved for musicians either; excellence in most things seems to increase appeal.

For companies this attraction represents the further necessity for excellence when trying to reach Gen Y consumers. For example, when Apple produces a product it is sexy. It doesn't need an Abercrombie & Fitch model to be standing next to it to be sexy. Apple's products are sexy on their own. The reason is because Apple strives for excellence in its products, and the company itself represents talent. Every step of buying a product from Apple shows striving for excellence. You enter the modern looking store and see all the cool looking machines. When you open your new Apple product even the packaging obviously has had a lot of attention paid to it.

Apple's attention to detail is similar to the musician who considers every last detail when writing your favorite song. A musician writes a song so that you enjoy every part of it, the words, the guitar solos, the chorus, and so on, that's why it is your favorite song. If the musician only made half of it good, you wouldn't love the song and wouldn't be able to overlook the lead singer's dumbo ears to find him or her attractive. To be attractive you must display talent every step of the way.

3. Hot for Teacher

It is not uncommon for students to develop crushes on their teachers. Maybe you have entertained your own academic-based fantasy at some point. If you have, you probably know that these attractions often have very little to do with appearance. Once again not too many teachers were confronted with the difficult choice between lucrative modeling contracts or a career in teaching. I think most would choose an after-party in Paris over a PTA meeting. However, despite their physical shortcomings, many teachers still manage to enrapture their students with daydreams.

One of the reasons for the teacher attraction is because smart is sexy. Especially with Gen Y, who highly covet intelligence, being smart is

Companies can appear smart by creatively solving problems, or innovating their workplace.

virtually a prerequisite for being considered sexy. This is good news for businesses because it's much easier for a company or a product to appear smart than many of the other attributes of attraction. Moreover, the opportunities for appearing smart are seemingly endless for both companies and products. Products can be smart because they cleverly fill a need, or perhaps are better designed than competing products. Companies can also be smart in manufacturing their products by being made through sustainable practices as discussed in Chapter 12.

Companies can appear smart by creatively solving problems, or innovating their workplace. For example, recently many companies have come to incorporate a new work model called ROWE, meaning a "results-only work environment." Essentially, workers are assigned tasks and deadlines and as long as their work is done on time they have no requirements placed on them, like having to be in the office from 9:00 to 5:00. This new work model acknowledges that thanks to technology many of the tasks that formerly required an employee to be in the office can be done by proxy, employees still have the option to come into the office and most do for at least part of the day, but they are not required to.

A smart managerial decision like ROWE makes the company seem more appealing, both for workers as well as consumers. Obviously employees would find this model appealing, because having to fight traffic every morning to go to an office to sit around bored half the day is wasteful and outdated. For Gen Y consumers, this work model makes the company more appealing. Gen Ys admire a company that is smart enough to make a logical management decision in order to make their employees more happy, and hence they are more likely to frequent this business. Being smart and innovative will attract better Gen Y workers as well as consumers.

4. Wanting the Unobtainable

An immutable law of attraction is wanting what we can't have. Many have felt the effect of this on their personal life. Many of my friends have griped about how when they are in a relationship everyone wanted them, but when they are single suddenly everyone has lost interest. Essentially this plays on the basic rule of economics that scarcity breeds value. Why is a diamond worth thousands when a piece of coal is almost worthless? Because there are a lot less diamonds going around than coal, and with diamonds being harder to acquire it makes them more valuable in the minds of consumers.

This is actually a great way of sparking Gen Y interest, because with the proliferation of the Internet, companies have all worked tirelessly to make every product abundantly available to the Gen Y consumer. However, many have done so at their own peril since in doing so they are ignoring this fundamental principle of attraction. Creating shortages in demand amongst consumers has time and time again been able to create frenzied purchasing spells; for example, with Gen Ys there was the Tickle Me Elmo, Furbys, and the Wii. Having grown up in a world where everything is plentiful thanks to the Internet, scarcity now has the power to attract Gen Y consumers more than availability.

When we apply the principles of the sexiness of talent, intelligence, and scarcity we can finally begin to form an overall sexiness. At the end of the day, the principles that drive attraction in person-to-person relationships can also be used to appeal to Gen Y consumers. This is important because in a crowded marketplace it becomes harder to be the loudest voice in the mob.

Savvy companies figure out ways to change how Gen Y consumers perceive them so that the Gen Y customers will actually seek them out. This ultimately is the tipping point for reaching Gen Y consumers: You can be the guy who goes out to the bar every night trying to meet girls, or you can be Hugh Hefner and have them come to you by the thousands all while wearing a robe all day long!

seventeen
CONSIDER THE SOURCE: USING ETHICAL PRACTICES TO ATTRACT GEN Y

Gen Y supports companies they feel are morally and ethically sound. One way to show Gen Y your company is ethically responsible is by only choosing to do business with companies that are fair-trade certified. Also, businesses that do grow or manufacture products can work to meet all the requirements to be fair-trade certified themselves.

Fair trade is a fairly new movement that seeks to make the business practices fairer to farmers and workers in developing nations, as well as ensure the quality of the products. This movement works on two principles that are very important to Gen Y. First, Gen Y is very world-minded, far more than previous generations they consider themselves more as citizens of the world over any one country specifically. Second, Gen Y is concerned about sustainable business practices that continue to be beneficial to both parties well into the future. Many of the unethical practices that spawned the fair-trade movement were very one sided and totally unsustainable. These practices were the modern equivalent to plundering and pillaging the already underprivileged. As a result many of the regions that were exploited for inexpensive resources over the last 50 years have become increasingly destabilized, and living conditions have dropped accordingly.

1. Examples of the Injustices Fair Trade Seeks to Correct

There are many practices that have become depressingly common in exploiting developing world resources. Many of these practices were able to flourish from a lack of oversight and governance, only now are these unethical practices being brought to the consumers' attention and, thanks to Fair Trade Acts, are finally being remedied.

1.1 Unethical labor practices

Many think of the idea of slavery as something that was ended by Abraham Lincoln. Unfortunately for millions of workers worldwide, the US Emancipation Proclamation is not doing them much good. In developing nations, slave labor, or situations similar to slave labor, is still a common practice. That is how many companies are able to keep their costs so low. When a company pays the workers very little or nothing it is easy to undercut competitors.

Even the practice of exploiting child labor is still a fairly common practice in many developing nations. Especially in agriculture the use of child labor is still very much widespread. Children are routinely forced to work 12-hour days picking produce. A recent study published in *Forbes Magazine* showed that on a cotton farm in Southern India as many as 54 percent of the workers were younger than the age of 14.

1.2 Unfair wages and pricing

Another unjust practice that fair trade seeks to correct is paying unfair wages or underpaying farmers for their harvests. Even when businesses do pay their workers they pay them such a low wage it is barely enough to pay for food and shelter. In the example of the cotton farm in Southern India workers were being paid only 20 cents an hour for their backbreaking labor.

Another common practice that often leads to workers being underpaid is when companies refuse to pay a fair-market price for products. The general mind-set of business schools the world over is to buy low and sell high. Often companies will get carried away with this principle and end up negotiating with farmers in developing nations to sell their crop for a ridiculously low rate, far less than the fair-market value. The problem with this is that it ends up affecting the lifestyle of the farmer and all their laborers. Ultimately if the farmer is not being paid a fair price for his or her crop, the person won't have the money to pay his or her workers a fair wage. Fair-trade organizations regulate this to ensure that companies don't underpay their providers so severely that they are unable to maintain a decent lifestyle.

1.3 Unfair hours of work

Another aspect of abuse fair trade curtails is unfair work hours. In many countries a 12-hour workday, seven days a week is more common than not. Obviously under these conditions the line between "worker" and "slave" begins to blur slightly. Workers must only be required to work 40 hours a week for a company to be considered for fair-trade certification, which is considered common sense in North America but in developing nations hours have to be diligently observed to ensure employees don't feel they need to work more than a fair number of hours a week to keep their job.

1.4 Poor health and safety standards

Not surprisingly one category that is consistently problematic for workers in developing nations is working conditions. Safety standards in many workplaces are virtually nonexistent as workers are often viewed as an easily replaceable commodity. Perhaps even more dismissal are the health standards, as you can imagine sick days are not exactly a prerequisite in most developing nations. As a result, if someone is sick the person will likely keep going to work anyways often exacerbating easily treatable conditions to the point of real damage. Likewise, when individuals are so sick or injured that they are unable to work they are just replaced and they are left with no means to support themselves or their families.

It is very depressing to consider the conditions most people in the developing nations are subjected to as they try to make enough money to support their families. The good news is that it doesn't require a lot of money to make these systems more fair and balanced, and Gen Y is committed to making that happen. Gen Y is willing to pay a little more or go a little out of their way to help correct many of these heinous practices.

For companies, it is important to realize just how much good comes out of fair-trade certification. Aside from promoting a more socially responsible image, supporting fair-trade initiatives is important. It is important to ensure that all people are guaranteed a certain quality of life. Condemning people in developing nations to live in poverty and hardship just so others can save a few cents on a pound of bananas is unthinkable. Gen Y is acutely aware of this and will definitely respect any company that is committed to making a difference.

Employees are most productive when they are happy; moreover, employees tend to care more about the state of the company they work for when they feel that the company cares about them.

2. Making a Difference at Home

Although the examples from developing companies may be more shocking, there are plenty of stories of workers being mistreated right here in North America. Many companies have forgotten that they have only two reasons to exist. The first is to keep the customers happy. The second duty of a business is to keep its employees happy. Doing this actually has huge ramifications for businesses. Employees are most productive when they are happy; moreover, employees tend to care more about the state of the company they work for when they feel that the company cares about them. However, for the intent of this book we will focus on the marketing value of having well-treated employees.

2.1 Profit sharing with employees

One way companies have been able to increase employee satisfaction and make them feel like more of a part of the organization is profit sharing. This makes sense if employees are working every day to make your company a success. Why shouldn't they enjoy some extra reward once the company is successful? This causes employees to feel more like actual parts of the organization and not just people who work for it.

One company that had a lot of success with profit sharing is WestJet, an airline in Canada. WestJet was able to differentiate itself by marketing that the company is employee-owned. Consumers make the logical assumption that if its employees have a stake in the company's profits, they try harder than employees who are solely on an hourly wage. Plus, West-Jet was also able to express to customers its dedication to its employees.

Gen Y likes companies that profit share with employees because we feel that most companies don't care about their employees or appreciate all the hard work they put in day after day to make the company successful. This is an especially good way for small companies to differentiate themselves from their larger competitors. Profit sharing shows you care about your employees. This is important because most of Gen Y are employees somewhere and we would sure appreciate it if we were treated better, so we will go out of our way to support a company that is trying to be part of the solution, not the problem.

Especially within Gen Y's short life, we have seen companies treat their employees worse and worse every year. Laying off employees after decades of loyal service, slashing benefits to appease the shareholders, it seems like every day big companies care less about the very individuals that make the business possible. As a result, Gen Y is more hypersensitive about how companies treat their employees. Instead of cutting benefits to employees, adding or increasing benefits is a great way to stand out from your competitors.

Often it is not even about the size of the gesture as much as it is about a company making any gesture at all. For instance, I recently saw a story about a mid-sized company that switched its cafeteria food to organic products to help employees stay healthier. First, it is noteworthy that the gesture actually made the news. It just goes to show how few companies try to make their employees' lives better. It is also noteworthy in that it is not a very grand gesture. The act of switching from regular food, which could contain harmful pesticides, to a menu that is free of toxins, doesn't exactly cost the company a lot of extra cash. It was not the extra money spent that the employees appreciated as much as it was the thought that the company cared about its employees' health and happiness. The company was willing to take steps, however small, to make the employees feel better. Not only does this send a positive message to the employees at the company it also sends a powerful message to Gen Y consumers. Topics like this tend to spread like wildfire throughout the Gen Y community.

I am acutely aware that Trader Joe's is said to treat its employees very well; whereas Walmart's reputation is that it treats its employees very badly. I didn't have to seek out this information through exhaustive amounts of research on the Internet, because friends reinforce it to me every time I go to buy groceries. "Don't shop at Walmart, it doesn't pay its employees a decent wage and it doesn't even give the employees decent health insurance," my friends remind me. As a result I do shop at Trader Joe's instead of Walmart, because I do want to promote companies that treat their employees well. I certainly don't want to be a person who has to work for a company that treats emplyees badly, so why would I support it by giving it my money?

At the end of the day, Gen Y is used to seeing companies exploit the "little guy" to expand their profits. This affords companies a great opportunity to show that they are in fact ethical and that they care about their employees and how their suppliers are treated. Gen Y will consistently award companies that care about others by caring about them. Ultimately, it is just a good practice all around. Cutting corners to save a couple dollars at the expense of other people's livelihood is unjustifiable. Nobody would condone the practices of child labor or unsafe working conditions. By buying only from fair-trade providers you can help put an end to these practices and gain more Gen Y customers in the process.

LONGWOOD PUBLIC LIBRARY
800 Middle Country Road
Middle Island, NY 11953
(631) 924-6400
mylpl.net

LIBRARY HOURS

Monday-Friday	9:30 a.m. - 9:00 p.m.
Saturday	9:30 a.m. - 5:00 p.m.
Sunday (Sept-June)	1:00 p.m. - 5:00 p.m.